Marie Demker

Colonial Power and National Identity

Pierre Mendès France and
the History of French Decolonisation

Göteborg Studies in Politics 109

Santérus
Academic Press
Sweden

www.santerus.se

All rights reserved. No part of this publication may be reproduced, stored in a retrieval system, or transmitted, in any form or by any means, electronic, mechanical, photocopying, recording, or otherwise, without the prior written permission of the publisher, except in the case of brief quotations embodied in critical articles and reviews.

The publisher has no responsibility for the persistence or accuracy of URLs for external or third-party internet websites referred to in this book, and does not guarantee that any content on such websites is, or will remain, accurate or appropriate.

Göteborg Studies in Politics 109

© 2008 Marie Demker and Santérus Academic Press Sweden
ISBN 978-91-7335-010-5
Layout: Harnäs Text
Cover photo: © Kamerareportage Bildbyrå i Göteborg AB
Cover profile: Sven Bylander
Santérus Academic Press is an imprint of
Santérus Förlag, Stockholm, Sweden
academicpress@santerus.se
Printed by BOD, Germany

Contents

ACKNOWLEDGEMENTS • 7

1. AN UNDERSTANDING OF INTERNATIONAL POLITICS AS IDENTITY CONFLICTS • 11

2. THEORETICAL AND METHODOLOGICAL CONSIDERATIONS • 16
    2.1 Constructivism as research perspective • 17
    2.2 Identity and identity crisis • 19
    2.3 How to analyse a discursive order – the analytical model • 22
    2.4 Why France? • 26
    2.5 How to do it • 27

3. FRANCE IN AN IDENTITY CRISIS? • 30
    3.1 Analytical tools • 32
    3.2 National Identity: Arguments • 34
    3.3 National Identity: Discourse • 40
    3.4 National Identity: Foundations • 52
    3.5 France in an identity crisis? • 56

4. PIERRE MENDÈS FRANCE AS PART OF THE FRENCH FOREIGN POLICY ELITE • 58
    4.1 A conventional career? • 59
    4.2 What was Pierre Mendès France's network? • 62
    4.3 Who were the opponents? • 64
    4.4 Which were the cleavages? • 65
    4.5 Pierre Mendès France and the French self-image • 67
    4.6 Mendès France's network and French self-image • 69

    4.7 Opponents outside the Radical Party:
        Guy Mollet, Robert Lacoste, Antoine Pinay and Joseph Laniel • 71
    4.8 Opponents within the Radical Party:
        Edgar Faure, René Mayer and Léon Martinaud-Deplat • 75
    4.9 Conclusion • 78

5. **PIERRE MENDÈS FRANCE AND THE CONCEPTION OF FRANCE • 81**
    5.1 What is a conception of France? • 81
    5.2 Conceptions of French identity: Arguments • 84
    5.3 Conceptions of French identity: Discourse • 86
    5.4 Conceptions of French Identity: Foundations • 91
    5.5 Conclusion: Pierre Mendès France
        and the conception of national identity • 95

6. **NATIONAL IDENTITY AND FRENCH INDOCHINA-POLICY 1954 • 98**
    6.1 From French Indochina to the American war in Vietnam • 99
    6.2 The year of 1954 – Defeat and surrender • 101
    6.3 The year of 1954 – the success of Mendès France • 105
    6.4 The year of 1954 – the aftermath • 110
    6.5 Conclusion • 113

7. **NATIONAL IDENTITY AND FRENCH NORTH
    AFRICA POLICY 1954–1956 • 115**
    7.1 From a "war against pirates" to an independent Maghreb • 116
    7.2 The year of 1954 – one step forward and two back • 118
    7.3 The year of 1956 – steps along another pathway • 128
    7.4 Conclusions • 132

8. **NATIONAL IDENTITY, DISCOURSE AND POWER • 136**
    8.1 Why did Mendès France succeed in Indochina
        but fail in Algeria? • 137
    8.2 National identity – a discursive order • 140
    8.3 How can national identities influence foreign policy? • 143
    8.4 Epilogue • 145

ARCHIVES: CONSULTED PRIMARY SOURCES • 148

REFERENCES • 150

Acknowledgements

After finishing this book I would like to express my gratitude to some people and institutions that made it possible. M. Dominique Franche at the Pierre Mendès France Institute in Paris has been very collaborative, and I have spent three research periods among the papers, books and journals in this well-organized archive. My possibilities to spend long periods in Paris have been facilitated by several weeks at the Centre Culturel Suédois in Paris. Without the generous economical support from Magnus Bergvall Foundation, Lars Hierta Foundation, the Royal Society of Art and Sciences in Göteborg and Karl Staaff's Foundation this book had never been accomplished.

I deeply thank Ph.D. Hans Andersson, Professor Bertrand Badie, Professor Ulf Bjereld, Associate Professor Ann-Marie Ekengren, Professor Lennart J Lundqvist, Ph.D. Ulrika Möller, Professor Bo Rothstein and Ph.D. Ann Towns for giving me the opportunity to have their comment on a draft manuscript. I would also like to thank our Seminar in International Politics at the Department of Political Science, Göteborg University for their valuable comment on parts of the manuscript. And, of course, Ph.D. Jasmine Aimaq, whom I met during my research in Paris; you did a great work with my English.

At the IPSA conference in Quebec, Canada, 2000, three people made small but significant contributions to my work. Professor Lois Wise took my paper up in her panel, Ph.D. Jacques C Hymans shared experiences from his research in Paris and PhD-candidate Lucile Desmoulins became a Paris friend with whom I discussed archives and literature.

Among other people also Ph.D. Patrik Stålgren, Ph.D. Johannes Lindvall, Ph.D. Carl Dahlström and PhD-candidate Andreas Johansson

Heinö had valuable comments on my work and Professor Maud Eduards gently offered me some academic papers from her earlier career, when she was studying the politics of Pierre Mendès France.

Most of all though, I would like to thank my family; my husband Ulf, my son Axel and my stepdaughters Anna and Ylva for their concern for me, interest in my work and patience with me both during my many travels and with my, sometimes no less than, obsession with French decolonisation.

Marie Demker

A l'intérieur d'un déterminisme historique fondamentale – qui, sur la très longue période, me paraît contraignant – les hommes qui contribuent à former l'opinion publique, et qui ensuite sont investis des responsabilités, ont des moyens d'être utiles ou nuisibles. En ce sens, il n'est pas sans intérêt de réfléchir à l'influence positive ou négative qui a pu être celle de tel ou tel homme.¹

Pierre Mendès France
1976

---

1   Quoted in Lacouture 1981. "Within the frame of a fundamental historical determinism – which I, in a long-term perspective, find compelling – individuals, who contribute in forming public opinion and debate, and who are also authorised to take on official duties and responsibility, are able to be useful or harmful. In that sense, it is worth reflecting on what kind of positive or negative impact this or that individual has pursued." *(Authors translation)*

1.
An Understanding of International Politics as Identity Conflicts

Why did France grant Indochina independence 1954 but deny the same status to the North African territories? Why did it take eight more years and thousands of dead civilians and soldiers before Algeria got its independence?

Indochina and Algeria are two processes of decolonisation, in many ways more similar than different, yet in the first case France entered negotiations, which led to independence, and in the second, there was not any place for negotiations. In both cases there was a pressure for national independence. Why did France act so differently in one case of territorial secession than in the other?[1]

The most common explanation among historians would highlight the existence of a national sentiment that made independence acceptable in the case of Indochina, but not in that of North Africa. National sentiments are not founded in a vacuum, however; they are, in the foreign policy context, also an outcome of policy processes, which include ideas regarding national identity and discussions among foreign policy elites. These discussions and this policy formation are grounded in national myths and national opinion. The existence of conflicting identity conceptions and

---

1   Another perspective is to deny the similarities between the two cases. Indochina could then be seen as a military failure after years of war, when Algeria was just in the beginning of a war to come. France gives therefore up Indochina but tries to take revenge through Algeria. But this perspective denies that North Africa – and Algeria specific – had been the scene of several uprisings since 1945 (exactly as Indochina). And it also denies that the war in Indochina had been a low intense conflict (and with French professional troops only) during a couple of years, with irregular outbreaks. I my view these two conflicts has more in common than they differ. See also the empirical chapter six and seven in this book.

conflicting individuals in decolonising France are here investigated and applied as examples for developing an analysis of foreign policy outcome focused not on information processing or beliefs, but rather a model of discursive structures and therefore a serious challenger to the traditional rational actor-model, as well as to mainstream constructivist approaches.[2]

In the decolonisation literature there are both rationalistic approaches and constructivist approaches. Among the most common explanations of decolonisation are changes in global power structures, efforts of independence movements and imperial overstretch. These three approaches share the assumption that state behaviour is best explained with reference to certain objective interests. These interests give rise to cost-benefit analyses, which in turn determines state behaviour – to withdraw, or not.

For historian H.L. Wesseling decolonisation was inevitable. Despite this he tries to define why it did happen when it did and how. He argues that the Second World War has weakened Europe so much that it had to be restored after the war, a goal that could not be reached with the colonies, only without them. He also argues that the process of decolonisation was determined by if the colony being occupied or not by the enemy.[3] But this argument does not answer the question why two more or less occupied territories (Algeria and Indochina) did get independence at different occasions. Historian Tony Chafer highlights the push-pull-mechanism between Paris and the federal French union government in West Africa to explain why the West African colonies choose independence and not further association. His conclusion is that personalities and political power struggle were more important than principles.[4]

A political scientist, Miles Kahler, has supposed that the internally divided France at the time of decolonisation gave way for a foreign policy that also maintained these divisions. Ideology was an interpreting tool for the colonial uprisings and the party splits inside parliament became deeper through the decolonisation process.[5] But even if Kahler makes sense of why Britain gave India independence in 1947 and France went to war in Algeria, it is not understood how and why Algeria and Indochina differed so much.

While important, these rationalist explanations suffer from a series of shortcomings. Most of the nations in our world should today refuse to use slavery even though it was presented as effective, profitable and well organised. There are several values and norms that restrict state behaviour

---

2   As examples Allison 1971, George 1980, Adler 1997.
3   Wesseling 1997.
4   Chafer 2002.
5   Kahler 1984.

and these have been given a more systematic account in the constructivist approaches. Constructivist approaches of decolonisation focus on international politics as fundamentally a matter of norms, identity and shared knowledge. The most prominent constructivist approaches are loss of imperial will, internally restructuring inside the colonial powers and new norms or new discourses in the international society. These approaches share the assumption that state behaviour is best explained with reference to common social behaviour and ideas.

In my opinion also constructivist approaches has shortcomings, namely that none of them systematically integrate mechanisms for explaining how and when decolonisation take place. In the long run France became a European power from 1954 until 1962, surely also because of changing norms. But why was then not all territories granted independence at the same time and already around 1950? None of the constructivist approaches has fully explained how and when a decolonisation process takes place.

Political scientist Robert H Jackson argues that the normative anti-colonialist framework grew out of the Second World War.[6] But he does not explain why India was granted independence in 1947 but Algeria in 1962. Economic historians and geographers Robert Aldrich and John Connell – although not constructivists – argues that the nationalist sentiments in the third world and the decline of ideological differences in world politics was the causal processes for de-colonisation.[7] But these explanations could neither answer the question why independence takes place at a given time and through a given process.

Other explanations of French decolonisation have highlighted that North Africa, in the Sahara desert, hide great oil resources. But they were not yet discovered and exploited in the beginnings of the 1950s. Sahara also became the place where France tested atomic bombs in 1960, but this military weapon was not either yet materialized. The most common explanation is the particularistic explanation that puts its force on the French demand for grandeur. France needed its territories over-seas to maintain its global power. But why did then Indochina – with its extremely strategic position – got independence but not Algeria, which did not has a global position? The answer is commonly said to be "the military was defeated in Indochina". Surely they were defeated, but it was the French democratic government – not a military regime – that after international negotiations gave Indochina independence. Why then did the struggle in Algeria get on for years, long after that the military in war terms was defeated also there?

6   Jackson 1993.
7   Aldrich and Connell 1998.

My answer is that the most plausible explanation is about the conception of French national identity. Indochina was never as important in the powerful elite conceptions of French identity as Algeria was.[8]

My argument is though that in a France, preoccupied with defining herself (in an identity crisis), it was impossible to establish a new national identity and have it broadly accepted. Given his success in Indochina, Prime Minister Pierre Mendès France believed that his new ideas had indeed been accepted. In reality, however, his solution for Indochina only happened to be compatible with the power relations and discourse of a conventional national identity. In the case of Algeria, it became evident that his conception of national identity was in principle fundamentally incompatible with the powerful French national identity conception of the military and the conservative groups among the landowners and businessmen at this time. Being in charge of the economic and symbolic state power, and because of a weak parliamentary system, these groups could enforce their national identity conception on the solutions for Algeria.

Theoretically, the above response highlights power relations as decisive factors in identity explanations. As one of few in constructivist international politics, political scientist Janice Bially Mattern has pointed out how and why power structures are important even though a constructivist approach is used. She connects representational force, physical force and social construction thereby questioning the more or less naïve reflection between shared norms on one hand and equality in deliberation on these norms on the other.[9] Constructivism seldom treats power asymmetry systematically and therefore power and power structures often are left out of the identity explanations.

My contribution to the decolonisation literature is a systematic analysis of power and how power affects social constructions of national identity. This analysis is mainly built on a discursive reading and interpretation of how French decolonisation did proceed during the short period of the Pierre Mendès France government in 1954 and his period as minister in the Mollet government 1956. During this period Indochina was granted independence and the Algerian war begun.

---

[8] In a recent study Todd Shepard argues that the Algerian war made an end to the conception of a cosmopolitan French identity. Shepard argues that France absolved itself from the consequences of decolonization by giving up their ideas of republican principles. Shepard 2006. This argument though was already formulated several years ago in Azar 2001 who shows, very convincing, that the Algerian war shook the French identity in its foundations. None of these mentioned studies are interested in the questions of how and why, questions which is in the middle of this study.

[9] Mattern 2000, 2001, 2005, Jackson ed. 2004.

National identity as a scientific concept consists in my view of *foundations*, *discourse* and *rhetoric*, and an idea must be accepted by the discourse in order to enjoy acceptance in foreign policy decisions. An idea that is compatible at the argument level can indeed slowly alter the concept of national identity, bringing to light the limits of the discourse and showing that power relations are obsolete.[10] Altered foundation could also reshape the discourse and therefore also the arguments. Only in these two ways a new national identity conception – as a discursive order – could be collectively accepted.

In the following chapter I discuss my research design and analytical perspective in detail. In Chapter Three and Four, I investigate and analyse identity conceptions in the French public as well as in the foreign policy elite. I then focus on the identity conception of Pierre Mendès France (Chapter Five), mainly through an analysis of his collected writings. The purpose here is to demonstrate when and where Mendès France's conceptions ceased to correspond to the national conception, and thus begin to outline the limits of his impact. In Chapters Six and Seven, I discuss the two cases at hand, Indochina and Algeria, and conclude the study in Chapter Eight with broader theoretical stipulations.

---

10   This discussion about results will be both evaluated and developed in the last chapter. In this section it has the function of pointing at a tentative conclusion.

2.
Theoretical and Methodological Considerations

National identity and foreign policy are intertwined. Foreign policy upholds and nurture national identity, and national identity constrain and motivate foreign policy. Foreign policy of a specific country normally reflects and considers a common understanding of national identity.[11] But how, and when, is it possible to impose a new foreign policy that demands a change of national identity? And how powerful are the ideas and the political force of a political leader, an individual, in that process?

Alexander Wendt explores the international system from a constructivist angle and declares that the international system is a social and cultural system where states view each other in different roles. He also focuses on driving forces that change the system, for example interdependence and a conception of common fate. His analytic focus though is on the system-level. In his book *Social Theory of International Politics* he explicitly argues that, in opposition to international politics, foreign policy has a tradition of studying how power and interest "are constituted by ideas" and he throws the glove by saying that "(I)t would be interesting to explore what, if anything, a more self-consciously constructivist approach might add to this approach".[12]

I hope that this study can help develop a framework for better understanding how national identities influence international politics, and thus

---

11 Goldstein & Keohane 1993:5–6, Katzenstein 1996:22, Rhodes 1999:70–71, Wendt 1999:163–164.
12 Wendt 1999:371.

also a better general understanding of foreign policy outcomes.[13] Through an empirical investigation of French national identity and decolonisation policy during the 1950s I argue that the constructivist perspective have to be supplemented by a systematic analysis of power before it can be convincing.[14]

2.1 Constructivism as research perspective

Constructivism differs, although it is not a homogenous perspective, from conventional perspectives in both premises and research themes. In constructivist research preferences are not taken for granted, they are looked upon as socially constructed, something contingent and possible to change. This does not determine an ontological anti-materialist assumption. Instead the constructivist agenda lean on Immanuel Kant who stressed the fact that our understanding of the world is formed by time and space – both are humanly constructed categories – but that does not imply that there are no (essential) things at all. Instead the ontological issue could be left out and focus be set on the epistemological issue. Constructivism is a research perspective, but it is also a theory about knowledge and about the social world.[15] In constructivist research ideas and material resources are treated as mutually constitutive for a constructed reality, they are not opposites or alternates.[16] Explanations should therefore be treated as process-related, teleological, sequential, intentional and cyclic rather than one-sided causal or linear.

The term "conception" is therefore used for the result of the mutually constitutive process between material context and ideas. Conceptions of national identity are treated as contingent and changeable spread by individuals and ideologies, but – by the same token – also as fairly weighty and also firm anchored in a material context.

Most of the literature in the constructivist field treats power structures as something that is socially constructed, and concludes that they do not

---

13 In Geva & Mintz there are several texts which try to build bridges between traditional rational choice theory and cognitive approaches. However, the texts in the volume are not primarily empirical and the authors firstly try to illustrate theories rather than build or test theories.

14 Mattern (2005) argues that this perspective is a form of 'post-constructivism'. In my study though, Foucault's perspective is used without arguing about if and how mainstream constructivism could not comprise his discursive methods.

15 Berger and Luckman 1967. Also Searle 1995.

16 Hay 2002.

have any force of explanation per se. Others look at ideas and beliefs as something that could only supplement power as explanation.[17] Martha Finnemore explains the making and acceptance of norms through individual actions, but she does not discuss power relations.[18] The omission is remarkable since at least two of her case studies (UNESCO and development aid) are largely defined by power relations. I will argue that norms can not be seen as constructed solely by individuals or ideas, but are contingent also on power relations. Jeffrey Checkel argues that the internal administrative organization of the state determines whether an idea will succeed in a national system.[19] I will argue that a discursive order in society is as important as administrative constraints to the success of an idea.

I argue that constructivism here could take advantage of the work of Ernesto Laclau and Chantal Mouffe and also Michel Foucault who treats power as a discursive element. Laclau and Mouffe treat all social practices as discursive. Power is a necessary element in a society, they argue, and it creates a room where societal organizing and mobilizing are possible. But at the same time power restricts and constitutes these organizing and mobilizing processes. Laclau and Mouffe stresses that there are always several discourses at stake. The subject is therefore a subject in several positions and is also subject for a struggle between discourses.[20]

Michel Foucault, on the other hand, argues that power is detectable only through the discourse, which is the only structure we can explore through scientific means. The discourse has a restraining force and to change the discourse is only widening the discourse. There is no place outside it. But in my interpretation Foucault also give place for a struggle of discourses. The discourse is therefore both constitutive and an explanatory.[21]

In this study I am going to use a discourse analysis but I will treat Foucault as an inspiration rather than a scheme. I demonstrate how a constructivist model of national identity, as an explanation to foreign policy change could be developed, and how power can be regarded as a determining force in that process.

17 Checkel 1997a p. 12.
18 Finnemore 1996.
19 Checkel 1997b.
20 Laclau and Mouffe 1985. See also Bartelson 2001.
21 Foucault 1971.

2.2 Identity and identity crisis

Exactly what is "identity"? In the late 1990s, literature on identity in International Politics began to evolve into more or less of a sub-discipline of its own. Most of the writers and researchers in International Politics[22] consider identity as an elastic concept, perhaps too elastic. At its nucleus, however, identity involves a conception of property. Identity is traditionally equivalent to a quality, or a property, of an individual. Identity calls for a created social individual. I argue that identity therefore is tied to self-cognition. But identity is also, according to Erik Ringmar, a necessary criteria for interest.[23] Only as "somebody" can we want "something. Tied to this process is recognition, which serves identity as a constitutive mechanism.[24]

Identity is a concept built on an empirical distinction between "us" and "them." Often it is said that an individual's identity is a reverse image of "them." Identity is then a concept defined by what it is not, rather than by what it is. Identity is in some other cases defined as our conception of whom or what "I" or "me" is. But this conception is also shaped by a reaction to what is different, to what we are not.[25] In modern political science the concept emanates from Hegelian and Marxist suppositions that identity is not given from the beginning, but is formed in the course of interaction with others. An actor will develop an identity first when he/she has interacted with others and has gained recognition from them. The key to understanding identity is thus self-description or self-image. In this school of thought we also recognise both a focus on conflicting identities and a process of reshaping identities.[26]

From European philosophers we have learned that the self has shifted from being something in the innermost circle of an individual to a universal self, which has a being of its own. To equate an individual with a self is therefore not theoretically viable. Identity is from this perspective viewed as a constructed cognition open to change and revision. Interesting explanatory factors included in this process are common cognitions, concepts and ideas. One of the most interesting works in line with this perspective is written by Erik Ringmar, who, in a distinctly European

---

22 The concept has a long history in political science, but has been modernised by anthropology before coming inside the theoretical world of International Politics. See also Hudson 1997.
23 Ringmar 1996.
24 Ringmar 1996.
25 Discussion in Lundgren 1998.
26 Bartelson (in Statsvetenskapligt lexikon) 1997.

tradition, discusses the philosophical grounds for scientific identity explanations. His book on Sweden and the Thirty Years' War is a valuable study, primarily because its point of departure is the European school of thought.

Ringmar argues that an identity crisis is a necessary condition for an identity explanation. Only in the context of crisis can the search of identity be a determining factor, he says, because the driving force to reach recognition is the most fundamental for a national collective. I will argue that an identity crisis is actuality more of a problem for an identity explanation, since in an identity crisis there is no room for a new identity to emerge and effectively establish itself. National identity is in my view a collective phenomenon and when the collective (the citizens of the actual state) experiences a denied recognition there is – according to Ringmar – an identity crisis. The crisis is a fact when recognition is denied and the struggle between identities can begin. This is a formative moment for national identity. According to Jeffrey Checkel, different state structures determine how and if new ideas penetrate the collective.[27] In the same way an identity crisis in a democracy and in a kingdom with a sovereign monarch have different consequences for the national identity. My argument is that in a democracy and where the crisis comes from the outside (it is outsiders who deny the national identity), the national identity is more rigid and relies on old conceptions that maybe "rescued" the nation in earlier crisis. In a democracy where the crisis comes from the inside (struggles between citizens belonging to different social or ethnic groups deny the national identity) a struggle between national identity conceptions will take place, and the societal order will gain conceptions with are compatible with the existing power relations. In a democracy therefore identity is more responsible for continuity than for change.

In the following sections, I will discuss collective identity in terms of "national identity."[28] It is of course not possible to simply generalise a concept from an individual to a nation; national identity can, however, be viewed as a metaphor for a national "self." A national identity is not an aggregate of individual identities, but a conception of "we" that is accepted – and that is part of individual cognitions of the world – in a delimited community.

Identity can be seen as a sort of supra-value that, through various strategies, demands a certain type of action. But the essential problem with theories of identity is that an absence of identity is almost impossible. Can we exist at all without an identity? Or can a nation exist without an

27 Checkel 1997 a & b.
28 Compare discussion in Goldmann 2001 p. 67–71.

identity? Probably not. "National identity" is therefore near empty as a concept, as "national interest" also is. We know it is there, but this will not really help us understand why and when the actor did what he/she did, because the so-called explaining factor was there all along. But, for the same reason, in cases of identity formation – especially when considering nations and states – the concept can be useful in helping to explain a certain action within the context of a struggle to form an identity.[29]

For the concept of "identity" to be a useful tool for scholars of contemporary politics, we must move past the discussion that I call "... identity or not, which identity and whose identity ..." If there is at hand more than one concept of identity in politics, which of them will be the most salient when applied to the nation? Can the struggle between possible identities be seen as an equivalent to identity formation? And how could identity help us to understand the choice of policy actions?

Identity is identity is identity, to coin Gertrude Stein's phrase. But if we take the concept of identity seriously we must admit that there cannot be a single identity applicable to a whole nation, or a whole society or a whole anything else. Identity is in my view not an essentialist concept, but a discursive order in which we participate more or less.[30] We might find groups that feel very strongly that their conception of their nation is the right one, while they feel other groups' conception is wrong. This would indicate competing identities within one nation. But this struggle is held on a structural level where the citizen's individual behaviour (loyalty) and attitudes (national sentiments) is determining. A nation with several national identities is not necessarily a nation in some kind of crisis. Identities can be tied to special spheres where they can operate independently of each other. And this never ending struggle opens up for national identities to reshape. National identity is in this study understood as a discursive order.[31] This is to say that the ruling conception of French national identity determines what is say-able and which the rules are that decides which national identity utterances are legitimate in the field I am studying – French de-colonisation policy 1954–56.

---

29 For a good example of using the concept in this way, see Ringmar 1996.
30 Zehfuss 2001 discusses the concept of identity inside the constructivist framework and highlight several problem with this definition.
31 Jörgensen & Phillips 2000 p. 64. Discursive order signifies a social room where different discourses partly grasp the same terrain, but contest about the interpretation of this terrain. In a discursive order one discourse generally is hegemonic, but challenged from both arguments and power relations. See figure 2.1.

2.3 How to analyse a discursive order – the analytical model

There is a deep gulf between Michel Foucault and his scientific concepts on one hand and the empirical social sciences on the other that ought to be bridged. Andrew Chadwick – who claims he has one foot in history and one in political science – notice that post-modern thinking has had much greater impact on political theory then it has on what can be termed empirical studies.[32] Foucault, not being a postmodernist, has in political science had the same fate. In an excellent study of environmental policy the sociologist Maarten A Hajer says that "there is a need to devise middle-range concepts through which the interaction between discourses can be related to the role of individual strategic action in a non-reductionist way".[33] Hajer then develops a combination of a social-psychological model and Foucault's discourse perspective and develops an analytical perspective for the regulation of the ecological debate.[34]

Foucault established his vocabulary of discourse in the text "Les mots et les choses" in 1966. He there refer to the analysis of humans as "how things in general can be given to representation, in what conditions, upon what ground, within what limits they can appear in a positivity more profound than the various modes of perception".[35] In this text Foucault refers to Heidegger's idea of the world as given to man, not conquered by man. We are all thrown out in a world, which is given to us in a constant relation of care (die Sorge). He also refers to an intellectual trajectory where it is possible to detect and reveal structures and things without searching into the mind of a human being. Taken together, this is a perspective that points in a methodological and empirical direction that too few social scientists have followed. Mostly discourse analysis has been treated inside the discourse theory perspective. I argue that there is a possibility of using the discourse-concept as a point of departure for developing an analytical tool for the analysis and understanding of political ideas and basic political concepts, without accepting the ontological statements of Laclau's discourse theory. I will also distance myself from the primarily communicational perspec-

---

32 Chadwick 2000 p. 284.
33 Hajer 1995 ps 52.
34 The concepts "story-lines" and "discourse-coalitions" play an important role in his analysis. A story-line is a narrative which provides the actor with the possibilities to illustrate where her or his work "fits into the jigsaw" and a discourse-coalition is formed when previously independent practises are "being actively related to one another". Hajer 1995 p. 63 and 65.
35 Foucault 1970 p. 337.

tive, which is known from Norman Fairclough.³⁶ Petr Drulák, researcher in international relations, has in a study of the EU discourse provided us with tools for treating concepts from the IR-literature with discourse analysis.³⁷ In his study Drulák shows that the European integration is better understood as dynamic if we identify metaphors of cooperation, as "motion" and "equilibrium". The theoretical conclusion is a contribution to the study of international structure, where micro and macro analysis goes hand in hand. My aim, as for Drulák, is to make a contribution to the discourse analysis by combining discourse analysis with identity concepts and developing an analytical tool for empirical use in an analysis of ideas and concepts, on the foundation of Michel Foucault's perspective.

I will, as said above, treat national identity as a discursive order where several discourses can operate and struggle for hegemony. The discursive order is detectable through three levels. National identity – which then is a collective phenomenon – ought to be seen, in the tradition of the French Annales-school, as tiered. I would argue that national identity is expressed through three levels.³⁸ We have one fundamental level, which is not open to adjustments. Ferdinand Braudel compares this level to the bottom of the sea. This fundamental level is more or less impossible to analyse directly, because it moves so slowly that we are all elements of it ourselves. It might, however, be tracked through an analysis of power relations. Power relations among actors who are involved in the discourse may be seen as expressions of the foundations of identity. The fact that de Gaulle, as new Prime Minister, used his military position to end the revolt in Algiers in 1958, indicates the important position of the military in French identity.

The second level is the real discourse. A discourse can change, and expresses itself through its regulation of societal practice.³⁹ And it is through practice that the discourse can be illuminated. Discourse is therefore a kind of deep-sea stream, shaped by the bottom of the sea but also a force of its own, shaping the waves. De Gaulle's use of his military position Algiers in 1958 suggests a discourse that is authoritarian and favours order.

At the top, we have the articulated arguments, the waves. That is the level that is most commonly analysed. When de Gaulle commanded the

---

36   Winther Jörgensen and Phillips 1999, Howarth, Norval and Stavrakakis 2000.
37   Drulák 2006.
38   Braudel 1969 p. 112, Burke 1992 p. 57 ff, Fink 1989 p. 334 f. Braudel use the terms "L'histoire événementielle", "l'histoire conjoncturelle" and "l'histoire structurale ou la longue durée". For a theoretically challenging discussion see Doty 1997.
39   Foucault 1971. For an overview compare Jörgensen & Phillips 2000.

revolting men in Algiers to return to their barracks, he was treating them as subordinates and citizens at the same time. The argument in his action was: "It is I who exercises political power, and who will grant France its grandeur, so you may cease your revolt and return to your duties." Argument is primarily a consequence of power relations and discourse, and to study an argument outside of this context would not help explain its determining power.

In sum, we have a discursive identity concept that consists of three levels: foundation, discourse and argument. An analysis of these levels requires studying social practice including non-verbal actions (discourse) and rhetoric content (arguments). Through an analysis of rhetoric content, practice and power relations among the foreign policy elite, it is possible to, in a more or less general sense; identify the national identity that lies behind the articulated statements in foreign policy arguments.

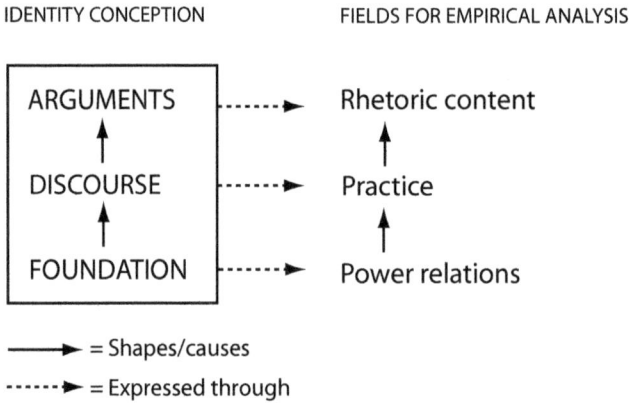

Figure 2.1 *The identity conception and levels of analysis*[40]

We know from earlier research that elite conceptions are extremely valuable as explanations for foreign policy actions.[41] To understand foreign policy actions by identity conceptions, we must identify the conception of national identity in the foreign policy elite. This identity conception would be the most determining in the formulation of national foreign policy.

40   I will discuss further methodological arguments in the section "How to do it".
41   For examples see George 1980, Wertzberger 1990, Singer & Hudson 1992, Checkel 1997, and Demker 1998.

Erik Ringmar points out that an identity explanation demands a state of identity formation period.[42] A struggle between competing identities is roughly the same kind of 'formative moment' as an identity formation period. I will argue that competing identities make an identity explanation less persuasive. If we state that elite conceptions of national identities are the most determinant in the selection of foreign policy actions, we must also admit that an unclear conception of national identity among the elite could be equivalent to an identity formation. Additionally, we know that in situations of great complexity individuals has a greater chance of having their conceptions determine the outcome.[43] This leads us to focus on individual positions to analyse whether a certain person could force his/her concept on the collective.

These two facts – that elite conceptions are most important and that great complexity improves the individual's chances of having an impact – allow us to draw a theoretical conclusion about identity. My argument is that if there is a struggle over identity among the foreign policy elite, the individual policy maker who effectively empowers his/her conception through power relations can successfully introduce his/her conception as the foundation of foreign policy. A struggle over policy is in that sense also a struggle among individuals over national identities. Conflicts about identity conceptions are almost always also discourse conflicts. In a power struggle the identity discourse is used to empower a certain identity concept.[44]

I argue that the effectiveness of identity conceptions as determinants in foreign policy is dependent on societal power. The identity conception is expressed through power relations, practice and rhetoric content. The discursive order, namely a conception of national identity, is stronger than particular ideas. If a new idea in foreign policy is to be implemented, it must be compatible with the discursive order, the identity conception, in society. If it is not, the policy strategy fails. If it is, the new idea might slowly reshape the identity conception by rendering the power relations or the arguments obsolete. These are elements in a theoretical framework with which I would like to supplement the existing literature.[45]

---

42 Ringmar 1996.
43 Allan 1994 and Gustavsson 1999.
44 Compare Rothstein 2000 who discusses the strategic incentives for an actor to influence collective memories in quite the same way as I do here about identity.
45 In Demker 1998 eight conditions were presented for an explanation based on a learning process to be at hand. Four of them are stipulated (few persons, a situation of formulating alternatives, demanding special skill, not a routine decision) and four are to be found in the empirical material (institutions generating ideas, policy entrepreneurs,

2.4 Why France?

In this book, I am interested in determining why Pierre Mendès France obtained approval for his foreign policy towards Indochina, but not in the Algerian case. Using the concept of identity, and focusing on the individual policy maker, how can we make sense of the success of the Indochina policy in 1954, and the failure in Algeria in 1955? In the mid-1950s, France was experiencing a sort of "identity crisis" amid the vivid memories of a nightmarish Second World War, immense welfare problems, and the dark legacy of the Vichy regime. I will attempt to show that there were competing conceptions of national identity among the French foreign policy elite at that time, and that these different identity conceptions were determinant to the outcome in Indochina and Algeria.

This study does not treat France or French de-colonisation policy as "cases" in a comparativist sense. Instead French de-colonisation policy is used to develop a theoretical thinking that could be used and improved through empirical research. I argue that Indochina was a threshold for France and national identity, while Algeria was the first instance in which the new policy could be implemented. France had not been very successful in her policy toward the colonies. Madagascar had witnessed a serious upheaval that ended in bloodshed. In Algeria, there had been numerous protests against French rule, and the Vichy-government and occupation of France had revealed weaknesses in the empire never before seen. In Indochina the nationalist movement had grown stronger during the Japanese occupation. After the peace treaty in 1945 in Europe, it was clear that France still had many fronts left to fight.

None of the other European powers had been occupied, playing the role of accessory and ally at the same time. France's painful status engendered serious doubts and questions regarding her position in the world. For Charles de Gaulle, – leader of "la Résistance," France had to become a great political power again; for Pierre Mendès France, France had to prioritize economic modernisation. For many intellectuals on Paris' Left Bank France ought first and foremost to live up to her national values of humanity and dignity, which should translate into a third world policy with de-colonisation and independence for all of the colonies.[46] For France, the 1950s were a decade of ideological cleavages, political weakness and colo-

---

real policy shift and presence of historical parallels). The argument in this paper are, although we are concerned with explanations to policy output and not to why a certain change took place at a certain time, a development of the results from that study. Through the more deep study presented in this book I hope to construct a model, not only come up with the conditions.

46 Azar 2000.

nial war – while France herself certainly was not clear on what "France" actually should be.

A study of the situation in France allows me to highlight a form of explanation that often has been overlooked by scholars. While colonisation and colonial power are not confined to a narrow period in European history, decolonisation came very abruptly, immediately after World War II, and also proceeded very rapidly. In the years from 1947 to 1960, nearly all colonised territories, with the exception of the Portuguese possessions, became independent. For France de-colonisation began with Indochina in 1954 and ended with Algeria in 1962, although France retains several minor territories still today. In eight years France lost all of her international "grandeur" at the same time as it was preparing for Gaullist economic modernisation. The process can be seen as an excellent example of a re-invented national identity. Other European examples might include Portugal after Salazar in the 1970s and Britain after the loss of India.

But France is particularly well suited to my study for several reasons. First, she found herself on both sides of the struggle during the World War. Second, there were clearly conflicting perspectives on de-colonisation among the elite in France, manifested through two colonial wars and internal upheaval nearly leading to a coup d'état. Third, she suffered from turbulent circumstances in domestic politics, with a succession of unstable coalition governments. These three conditions are significant if an identity explanation should prove to be fruitful. I have chosen France and French de-colonisation policy to a) show that identity can play an important role and b) determine the manner in which identity can serve as an explanatory factor. To that end, the case studies must be as illustrative as possible so that all steps in the chain of connections can be explicitly distinguished and formulated. Ideally, a subsequent study will examine this chain and test it with at least one case study that is not as obviously compatible with the theory as are mine.

2.5 How to do it

France withdrew from Indochina in August 1954 following negotiations among the nationalist movement, France, the United States and the Soviet Union. France left Algeria in July 1962 after an eight year war, deliberations between the nationalist movement and France, and a referendum in both France and Algeria. For both cases, I will show the reader that a special conception of national identity, carried by Pierre Mendès France, was instrumental.

In Indochina, France – and Pierre Mendès France – was confronted with a new sort of problem: how to cope with de-colonisation. My argument is that the Indochina case saw a shift in French foreign policy, where Pierre Mendès France launched novel ideas about national identity. He won acclaim among both voters and elite for his conception of French identity, and was able to negotiate on that foundation, knowing that his conception of French identity was accepted. When he was ready to solve the Algerian crisis on the basis of the same conception of French identity, the conception was no longer viable. He met with resounding opposition in the Assemblée Nationale and was compelled to resign. Why?

As discussed earlier, identity conceptions are in this study structured into three parts: foundations, discourse and arguments. These three levels can be studied through power relations, practice and rhetoric content. The simplest answer to the question above – Why? – is that Pierre Mendès France's conception of French identity was not compatible with his political adversaries' conception at each of these levels. Mendès France's arguments/rhetoric content was compatible with the mentality/discourse of the foreign policy elite's conception in the Indochina case. What he did not recognize was that the Algerian case was subject to a different discourse altogether, built on a separate foundation/power relations.

In this book, I will discuss why and how France was a nation experiencing an identity crisis, identify the foreign policy elite and the parliamentary elite directly involved in de-colonisation policy, and analyse the identity conceptions in the Indochina and Algerian cases. I will then trace

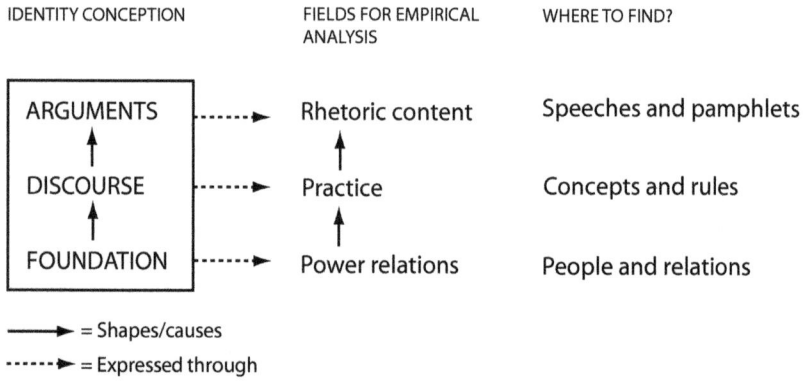

Figure 2.2 Operative scheme and research "material"

Pierre Mendès France's conceptions of France and demonstrate in which steps of the process his conceptions deviated from his adversaries. Finally, by using the conclusions of this study, I will discuss a possible approach for identity explanations for international politics.

My research consists in part on analyses of relevant debates and public speeches on both Indochina and Algeria. I have also explored political writings that were intended for the general public but also private papers and documents. My purpose is to characterise the arguments through an evaluation of rhetoric content. From these arguments, I will identity the central figures in the discourse and attempt to decipher the rules that keep certain things out of the discourse while allowing others in. Practice entails a wider range of material, but the arguments extracted from the rhetoric content can help to set useful limits. I have analysed newspapers, literature, social movements, opinion formations and personal writings. An exploration of concepts and rules should help reveal the nature of the discourse, enabling me to analyze both the people who actually "carry" the discourse, and also the more commonly observed foreign policy elite.

3.
France in an Identity Crisis?

As she resurrected after the Second World War, France was still an imperial power. But France had never, as Alfred Grosser writes in his classic study of 1961, "La IV'e République et sa Politique Extérieure," been confronted with as many challenges to her legitimate national status as during the post-war Fourth Republic (1946–1958).[47] In this chapter, I will argue that French citizens and political groupings spent the late 1940s and early 1950s engaged in a perpetual struggle over their national identity, an identity crisis.[48] The empirical support for this argument is that the official political *rhetoric* was filled with debates about national identity, that French popular *practice* was imbued with matters relating to identity, and that *power relations* among political parties, individuals and lobby groups reflected a struggle over identity questions.

Identity as an explanatory factor in French de-colonisation is not contingent on whether the decision-making process in the foreign policy elite was conducted in a national environment characterised by an identity crisis. What I mean is that an identity crisis represents a moment where individual actors can attempt to reshape national identity. Identity explanations are of interest whether or not an identity crisis is occurring. The key issue is to identify *which* national identity is at hand.

According to Ringmar, Pierre Mendès France should have been successful if France was in an identity formation period. I am going to argue that these years truly were identity formative (identity crisis), but that this situation made Mendès France's efforts to reshape French identity more, rather than less, difficult.

---

47 Grosser 1961:187.
48 I hereby make use of a political operative concept of a nation which comprise elites, citizens, parties and mass media.

3. FRANCE IN AN IDENTITY CRISIS?

To show the existence of an identity crisis in France during the first half of the Fourth Republic, I will use the same concepts as when analysing the elite debates in a subsequent chapter. In this chapter, however, I will of course draw from a separate body of empirical material. Since I am interested in identity conceptions on an aggregate level, this chapter requires empirical evidence different from that required in my subsequent discussions on identity conceptions within the elite. I have chosen to work primarily with printed media, opinion polls, political protest behaviour and parliamentary documentation. Figure 3.1 shows how my material relates to the different levels in the conception of national identity.

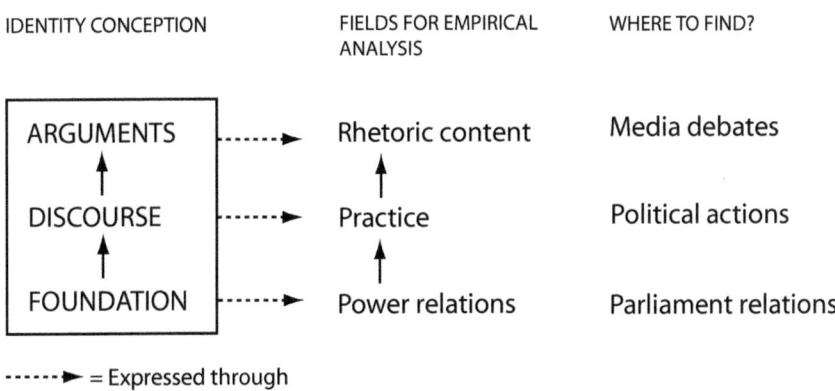

Figure 3.1 *Operative scheme and research material for analysing national identity at aggregated level*

Unsurprisingly, almost no one in the political debate explicitly makes use of the concept "identity." The latent message within the debates and practice must be deciphered. I therefore have to employ operative concepts and analytical tools to determine which media debates, practice and relations are linked to identity conceptions. This is intriguing work since both the concept "identity" and the material have somewhat fluffy perimeters. There are almost no examples of scholarly works that apply identity analysis to an empirical test case founded on thorough conceptualisations, operationalisations and a specific body of material. Through my analysis, I hope to demonstrate that an identity-explanation can be as viable as other, more common types of explanation.

3.1 Analytical tools

Identity is a concept which is usually linked to "who I am" or "who you are". Self-image is, as discussed in Chapter One, a core part of national identity. In this chapter, I will use self-image as an operative concept for finding – and demonstrating – that there was an identity crisis in post-war France. If the French citizenry and elite did not experience a crisis, I would hesitate to insist that a crisis was taking place regardless of their unawareness of it. And if citizens and elites were not conscious of the crisis, it seems very far-fetched to argue that the identity crisis was a determining factor in French foreign policy.

I have chosen to focus on newspaper debates to capture the French self-image on the argument-level. It seems reasonable to assume that, taken as a whole, these debates comprise an informed material in which the principal self-images of the era can be seen. I have chosen also to focus on social political practice, including analyses of elections and polls, to capture the self-image as it was reflected on the discourse level. Publicly and collectively stated attitudes and behaviour should provide insights into dominant popular themes, and should permit an overview of commonly held attitudes. I will work both with texts and vestiges of demonstrations, protests and rebellions. To analyse and capture self-image at the foundational level, I have chosen to focus on parliamentary debates and official statements made by those in power. Official material can provide a good map of power relations and of conflicts or consensus over national identity.

In my analysis of the above material, I will rely on the same textual tool, namely, a contextual interpretation guided by a two-step analysis of language.[49] When I work with practice I will analyse the vestiges as a kind of text, and will therefore primarily use the same method. To prove the existence of an identity crisis, it is necessary to show a plurality of identities at least in the discourse level (a necessary and sufficient condition), but my argument will be a great deal stronger if I can distinguish plural identities also at the other two levels. The plural identities must also be conflicting, which means that they are tied to the same spheres. If there are different identity conceptions at different levels in the analysis they could exist "side-by-side". To establish that France experienced an identity crisis I must support my thesis by showing both that the plural identity conceptions exist at the same level and that these conceptions are mutually exclusive.

Why is discourse the most prominent level in this analysis? Because the discourse level is where the political system has its legitimacy and where

---

49 Demker 1993 and 1997.

3. FRANCE IN AN IDENTITY CRISIS? 33

a collective national identity must be anchored in order to be called a "national" identity. If there is confusion on the other levels too, all the worse! If I am unable to demonstrate that there were multiple identity concepts at the discourse level or/and in the argumentative level, then perhaps there was no identity crisis after all. The foundational level is too stable to be useful as a test for falsifying my thesis; this analysis aims instead to support the point at the other two levels.

I will approach the text with a two-step formula. The first step consists of reconstructing the political context and identifying key-issues for the particular field. I then identify key words and key-arguments associated with the key-issues in the context. In the second step of textual analysis, I will link these key words to three dimensions of self-image: the self, the community and values.[50] All interpretations will be further discussed and argued in connection with the material.

A simplified analytical scheme is introduced in Figure 3.2. The properties of the analytical dimensions are: the limits of national self-perception ("us – them"), the limits of national community ("member – outsider") and the limits of national values ("inclusive – exclusive").

Self-perception:	US or THEM
National community:	MEMBER or OUTSIDER
National values:	INCLUSIVE or EXCLUSIVE

Figure 3.2 Analytical dimensions of the operative concept national self-image

In my analysis, I consider self-image as an indicator of, but not equal to, the theoretical concept of identity. Self-image is analysed through three dimensions, from the perception of the self in cultural terms, to the idea of belongings in one's own community, to the evaluation of the scope of one's own values. An image could be described as a "mental picture(s) composed of our cumulative experience-based "knowledge." A national self-image is consequently a mental picture of one's own nation based on knowledge from self-experience.[51]

Self-perception is the dimension where I search for how citizens define themselves as a unique people.[52] The relevant question here is how the "we French" is distinguished from "them". Is it on the basis of ethnicity,

50 Compare Skinner 1996 p. 7ff and Tralau 2001 p. 28ff.
51 Elgström 2000 p. 68.
52 Oommen 1997, Azar 2001 p. 10ff.

history, language, race, or citizenship? Or is there any other determinant factor? I will attempt to define the limits of "us," and whether there are many "us-es" in French society.

National community is the dimension where citizens distinguish themselves as a community.[53] A community could be defined as a group that is imagined to be historically tied together, a territory that has a political unity, or simply as a unit with political autonomy. Important here is by what criteria a member is defined, and by what criteria an outsider is defined. I will try to mark the limits of "France", and thereby address the question of whether there are many indeed "France" in France.

National values is the dimension where I search for how citizens conceptualise their own national values. There is an often-mentioned dichotomy between a universal and a particular conception of a nation, where the first is linked to the French Enlightenment and the second to German Romanticism.[54] If national values are comprehended as universal, they are not restricted to one's own community. This suggests a national self-image that is inclusive. A nation with an inclusive self-image could be inclined to perceive itself as having a "civilizing mission;" its values would be considered universal, rather than tied to a particular history or culture. If, on the other hand, national values are comprehended as unique or tied to the actual situation in one's own culture, or nation, the national self-image will be characterized by exclusion. A nation with an exclusive self-image could be inclined towards isolationism, since the nation's values would be linked explicitly to history, language or ethnic markers.

In this chapter, I investigate the French self-image as an indicator of French national identity in terms of arguments, discourse and foundations. On each level the issues of self-perception, community and values will be addressed.

3.2 National Identity: Arguments

By studying media debates that appeared in *Le Monde* between June 1953 and March 1955, I have been able to trace an underlying discourse in French society about French national identity. As mentioned earlier, I have chosen to discuss self-image as an indicator of national identity, and I have

---

[53] Eriksson 1997 p. 20 refers to "patriotic core values" and mention group identity, political autonomy and congruence. Also Smith 1991 and Anderson 1991 about nationalism. Se also Grendstad & Selle 1996 and Thompson, Grendsted and Selle 1999, Wardhaugh 2007 about communities and national values.

[54] Silverman 1992 p. 19.

broken down this concept into three levels: self-perception, national community and national values. All of these will be discussed here. The first noteworthy discovery I made was that of a total of 229 articles, 79 dealt explicitly with French identity. In other words, a third of all editorials (34 percent) were focused, in one way or another, on the simple question: "What is France?" I was very strict in my categorization and have only included articles that explicitly dealt with identity.

Self-perception, National Community and National Values

Le Monde was widely read by the political elite in France, and the arguments put forward in the articles were the most prominent in the public political rhetoric at that time.[55] I believe that these arguments not only reflected the public debate, but also influenced this debate by focusing it on particular themes and/or issues. The arguments are part of an identity discourse taking place at the time. The issues that were discussed were the European Defence Community and the Paris Agreements (33 articles), national economy and parliamentary politics (19 articles) and Indochina (9 articles). There is no doubt that the European Defence Community Policy (EDC), relations with Germany, and French imperial ambitions were the core identity issues during the period here under study (1/6 1953 until 31/3 1955). The frequency of editorials, which appeared under the heading "Libre Opinion," varies a great deal. There are at least six articles and at most 16 in a single month. The debate reaches culmination point between October 1953 and May 1954, the month before Pierre Mendès France came to power. No more than eleven articles appeared in any single month from June 1954 to February 1955, while, over ten articles appeared each month between October 1953 and May 1954. (See Table 2.1.)

---

55 Grosser 1961 p. 168.

Table 2.1 Articles under the "Libre Opinion" column in Le Monde 1/6 1953 until 31/3 1955.

Month/year	Frequency	Whereof identity related articles
June 1953	6	1
July	11	3
August	6	1
September	7	1
October	11	6
November	13	7
December	15	7
January 1954	13	4
February	10	5
March	15	3
April	16	5
May	14	6
June	9	3
July	9	2
August	10	5
September	9	2
October	9	3
November	11	5
December	9	1
January 1955	7	1
February	6	2
March	13	6

As can also be seen in Table 2.1, the number of editorials that contain identity rhetoric increases the general frequency of editorials does. This indicates that the relation between debate in general, and identity debate specifically, is stable, which can be seen also if we chronologically divide the period: in the period 1/6 1953 to 30/4 1954, we find that 35 percent of editorials deal with identity, in the period between 1/5 1954–31/3 1955, 33 percent do. The Pierre Mendès France period diverts thus distinct from the preceding period in terms of the intensity of the debate, but not in terms of the frequency of identity related articles.

Nearly all of the editorials here analysed (74 articles) address the dimension of "self-perception", while 64 articles address the dimension of "national community," and only 32 address the dimension "national values". I have chosen to have more than one mention for each article and therefore I have found 96 mentions of cultural categories answering the question "who are we?" within the "self-perception" dimension. History based cultural categorization and categorizations tied to nationalistic political issues appear most frequently. Ethnic, language, religion or international regional categories are of only minor importance. Results are presented in Table 2.2.

Table 2.2 Mention of cultural categories in French self-perception

Category	Frequency
History, nation	18
Geography, Frenchmen and ethnicity	15
Values	15
Class, power	13
Europe	10
French Union	10
Citizens, republic	8
Catholics	1

Comment: Based on 79 "Libre Opinion" editorials in Le Monde, 1/6 1953–31/3 1955.

I have chosen to group certain categories together, if they appear to rest on the same principle. For example, history had only three mentions, but nation had fifteen, class had five and power, eight. Which, then, are the arguments hidden within these cultural categories that reveal a "We" against a "Them"?

Within history and nation, we find arguments such as 'we were the ones who won the war', 'we are in opposition to all other European nations', 'we have to take back our role in politics' and 'we have a cultural scope that encompasses the entire world'. In the geography and ethnic categories, arguments imply that 'we are different than they are', 'we are French' (with some affectation) and 'we are French, they are Americans'. There is more a repudiation of others, rather than a glorification of "ourselves". Behind the category of values hide arguments of democracy, a unique (French) role in the political system and the belief in a civilising mission. When it comes to class and power, most of the arguments indicate dissatisfaction with the political elites in the French political system, or concerns about the shrinking role of France in world politics. The French "us" thus exists in a constant tension between geographical categories and value-based categories, yet there is no consensus about French identity. Different writers focus on different categories while different issues bring different categories into focus.

In the 64 editorials that discuss the dimension "national community" – addressing the question of "Who is a member (of the community)?" – I have found only one conception of "member" in each article. Most common is a conception of the people and the nation state. We then have a clearly citizen-based category where history or regional values do not play important roles. The findings are in Table 2.3.

Table 2.3 Mention of member categories of French national community

Category	Frequency
Nation State, the People	20
Political system	12
French Union	12
Ideology and values	11
Europe	9

Comment: Based on 79 "Libre Opinion" editorials in Le Monde, 1/6 1953–31/3 1955.

There is in French political rhetoric a prominent tradition of speaking in the name of "le peuple français," or the nation as such, but as we can see in Table 2.3 this tradition was challenged during the years under study. That is not to say that traditional rhetoric is the determining factor in defining the national community. It is more fair to say that both people based, political based and value based national communities were present.

Only in 32 of 79 editorials is the dimension "national values" addressed, and then only in one way in each article. Here we have a more homogenous picture of the articles declare that French values are inclusive, while ten state that they are exclusive. The inclusive picture is composed of arguments about French values as universal in both scope and time. Many of the articles focus on the obligation of France for the dissemination of a western value-dimension worldwide, and others underline France's position as a neutral power in between (or aside from) superpower tensions.

I have also conducted a minor study on the image of the world that is presented in the headlines. To avoid methodological problems, I have carried out a comparison with a Swedish case. I studied geographical locations appearing in the headlines of both *Le Figaro* and the leading Swedish newspaper, *Dagens Nyheter*, over the course of a single month (December 1954). There are striking parallels between them, which suggests that the world news, and not some particular French factor, explain why the editorials were so preoccupied with French identity. Table 2.4 shows the result of this analysis.

Table 2.3 Mentions of geographical locations (aggregated in categories) in the headlines on the front pages of Le Figaro *and* Dagens Nyheter, *December 1954, with percent of mentioned locations. (Only one mention per location and day)*

	Le Figaro	Dagens Nyheter	
Own country	24	24	
Superpowers	23	23	
North Africa	11	4	
Southeast Asia including China	14	19	
Nordic countries	1	7	(Sweden not included)
Europe as region	4	0	
Single European states	23	24	(France not included)
	N=131	N=75	

The results imply that the Swedish leading newspaper *Dagens Nyheter* (Today's News) was somewhat more interested in Southeast Asia than was France, at least if the news headlines are to be believed, despite the fact that France had just fought a war in Indochina.

Also noteworthy is the fact that *Dagens Nyheter* did not mark the outbreak of the Algerian war in November 1954 in its headlines. The two references to North Africa in *Dagens Nyheter* concern Egypt. I am not certain on how to interpret the fact that *Dagens Nyheter* named far fewer locations than *Le Figaro* in their headlines. Perhaps it is a natural consequence of the different readerships in the two countries, with the newspaper in Sweden being targeted to a broader public, whereas *Le Figaro* was read primarily by the elite in France and therefore has less of local interest on the front page. At any rate, my minor study indicates that French newspapers were not unique in their focus on the world, and that neither domestic nor foreign events can be viewed as situational explanations for the intense identity debate in France.

Conclusion

If we accept that national self-image, as discussed earlier, is an indicator of national identity, then we must concede that French national identity on the argument-level is neither clear nor homogenous. We have seen that on all dimensions of self-image, there are confusing arguments. The *self-perception* is divided between historically and nationally defined categories on the one hand and value, or power based categories on the other. The conception of who is a member of the *national community* is divided among membership on the basis of political, national or value foundations. Only in the conception of *national values* is there some homogeneity; most of the arguments claim that French values are universal. I will argue that the reason why this dimension (national values) appears so much less frequently in the editorials, i.e. n in only 32 of 79 articles, is that it was far less disputed than the dimensions of national communities and self-perception. I will conclude by asserting that I have revealed the existence of an identity crisis on the argument level in national French identity, and can therefore argue that one criterion for an identity crisis, although its fulfilment is neither necessary nor sufficient, has been fulfilled.

3.3   National Identity: Discourse

During the period June 1953 to March 1955, France experienced a wave of political and economic protests. Most of the extensive and serious strikes took place prior to June 1954, in other words, before Pierre Mendès France came to power. In contrast to the previous period, Mendes-France's Prime Ministership saw only two significant labour strikes/protests. I have chosen to focus on political behaviour within the labour market (mainly strikes), political demonstrations, opinion polls, and elections, as well as on the development of the economy during this period.

Referring back to Figure 3.2, I will interpret labour protests and relations as reflective of a self-perception where an "us" and a "them" are defined. In a way it could be said to be determined because of class relations, but it is my contention that the nature of the strikes and labour market relations at the time were an expression of deeper structures in France. This deeper structure is what I would label a societal discourse that is more broadly decisive to all citizens, than a contingent class structure.[56] Political protest, I argue, is also an expression of a discourse, but should be viewed

---

[56] I will not argue that class based politics is not relevant, only that societal discourse has a stronger impact and decides even class conflict expressions.

as more of a community-based expression. Through political protest and demonstration, citizens define their national community; protests usually are aimed at the political leadership. Opposition to the national leadership indicates a demarcation of the relevant community, and therefore is informed by membership vs. intrusion. In elections and opinion polls, the discourse is expressed through national values, both because political parties precede them, and as dimensions underpinning the citizens' choices. I will therefore interpret elections and opinion polls as indicators of national values in terms of either exclusive or inclusive.

The economy was plagued by negative development in 1953, and not only in France. The trade balance was negative in France, a trend that accelerated during the year. In 1954 the situation stabilised somewhat. Salaries rose, production increased and the trade imbalance were mitigated. The situation continued to improve in 1955. In France, many politicians saw the Korean War, which ended in the summer of 1953, as the impetus behind healthier economies in both the United States and Europe.

Strikes, demonstrations and elections/opinion polls from 1/6 1953 to 31/3 1955 provide a wide lens on the French discourse of the time. Most of the strikes were related to central sectors of national political and economic life, with wine producers, communications, white collar, school and agricultural workers all involved. I will analyse the major strike of August 1953, the wine and agricultural worker protests of autumn 1953, and the functionaries' strike of November 12, 1954. In addition, I will investigate the upheavals at Place Etoile on July 14, 1953 and in the Quartier Latin in November 1953. I will also rely on some opinions polls from 1953.

Self-perception: strikes

One of the major strikes of the period took place in August 1953. It began as an illegitimate protest at the local post office in Bordeaux, but soon escalated into a nationwide strike involving mainly the communications sector. The protest erupted after Prime Minister Laniel began talks on economical and social politics with a number of labour organisations. The trade union C.G.T, which was affiliated with the Communist party, demanded that their members at P.T.T (Post- and Tele Communications) organise an "action day" on the 4th of August, 1953. The C.F.T.C and F.O. (other trade unions) joined in, and, within days, the strike was nationwide. At August 7th, two million people were on strike, most of them communications workers in the postal, transport, electricity and gas sectors. Within a week the strike had expanded to the private sector. Initially, the main target of the striking workers had been the government, in light of new, unpopular pension rules and license requirements for lorry drivers, and in protests against a general economic policy that was seen as reactionary. Once the private sector got involved, however, the strike transformed into an "explosion of a general discontent".[57]

Prime Minister Laniel made efforts to negotiate with the trade unions, but many of the workers refused to listen to their organisations when these tried to put an end to the strike. On August 17th, Laniel threatened to cease all discussions if the strikes were not immediately halted. Tensions sharpened, and the government organised a massive police force to manage the demonstrators. A number of politicians, as well as the leaders of the trade unions, recognised the precariousness of the situation, and on August 21st, the three trade unions were officially received by July, the Prime Minister's Secretary for the State.

The government met almost all of the trade unions' demands, and also promised that there would be no sanctions against the striking workers. Bringing a definitive end to the strike remained difficult, however. It was not until the 25th of August that every worker was back on the job.

While the strike had been focused on salaries and regulations, the fundamental cause was general discontent within French society. Public opinion demanded change, although it was not clear exactly what sort of change. French society was in a sense a "blocked" (bloquée) society, where nearly half of the population had no political influence. The Communist Party (26.5 percent in the election 1951) was kept outside of every government, as was the Gaullist movement (21.5 percent in the election 1951). French politics were thus characterized by middle-ground parties taking turns at the highest ranks of power, which added to the frustration of the public, in the midst of a deepening quagmire in Indochina and weak economy at home.

In November 1953, school and university teachers went on strike as well. They were supported by parental associations, and appealed to allow schoolchildren to remain home one day of the week.

And in the spring of 1954 there were several strikes and so called "action days" where public discontent was evident. In March 1954, the trade unions began to discuss the need for wage increases. Most called for a higher minimum wage, but there were also demands for fiscal reform where social welfare would be paid out of, taxes rather than union fees. Among the white-collar groups, demands focused on individual salaries, no mediation in labour disputes and greater independence for civil servants in the nationalised industries. The employers' organisation was

---

57 L'Année politique 1953 p. 174.

more interested in liberalizing foreign exchange regulations. On the 28th of April 1954, the two trade unions C.G.T. and C.F.T.C initiated a 24-hour-strike. This time, however, the F.O did not wish to follow. The government responded by increasing the minimum wage, from which a new "wage ladder" was built, and by introducing differential salaries for teachers from primary school to higher education.

Other parts of the French Union also witnessed strikes. In Senegal, a general strike was held on November 3–5 1953 in protest against new labour regulations, and Tunis, there was a major strike among railway workers in January 1954. Labour market relations were thus tense not only in Continental France, but equally so in sub-Saharan and North Africa.

The measures taken to appease the situation did not end the discontent among civil servants and employees, however. Both C.G.T and white-collar trade unions demanded more. They claimed for higher wages, the reinstatement of hierarchical organisation, fiscal reforms, and educational reforms. The employees' organisations demanded new policies in almost every possible political field. Neither the employers' organisation nor the government was able to satisfy these demands. It was not until Pierre Mendès France was installed as prime minister in late June 1954 that the protests temporarily ceased.

New strikes erupted already in November 1954. Although the new government had legislated for a higher minimum wage, price reductions, measures to defend workers' purchasing power, national funds for industrial conversion, state credits with low interest rates for trade, business and industry, and special funds for trade and business that employed inactive members of the labour force, discontent remained. On the 12th of November, F.O and C.G.T together announced a strike in the public sector, primarily aimed at an increase in wages. Discussions with the government proved fruitless. In addition, harbour workers in Bordeaux had been striking since mid-October. By the end of November, it was clear that the situation in the labour market was precarious, despite the fact that French economy had recovered quite well during the autumn.

The state mediation law of 1950 had not been applied during the strikes of 1953–55, but on the 6th of January 1955, the Mendès France government proposed a new law, more modest than the enforcement law of 1950, and intended to facilitate the solution of labour conflicts. The institutionalisation of a mediation process was agreed to on the 5th of May 1955 – by the new government – and that process was already anchored in all labour organisations.

My interpretation of these labour market protests, rebellions and strikes is that although they were naturally focused on higher wages and better working conditions, they were primarily expressions of broader popular discontent. By galvanising employees, civil servants and workers – both in Continental France and in the French Union – in nation-wide strikes where political demands were as important as salaries, the labour force manifested a sense of "us-them" against the political elite, higher civil servants, and government. I therefore would argue that strikes indicate an identity issue in the French society. I cannot with certainty claim that the identity issue amounted to a "crisis", however, since the strikes galvanised people from many different groups against the government. The division between the people and the politicians can be interpreted as a challenge to the possibility of a truly united French nation.

If there had been a greater incidence of minor strikes, professional-based strikes, or sporadic strikes and protests, this interpretation might not seem viable. It is also plausible that the temporary interruption of major strikes when Pierre Mendès France took over as prime minister indicate that earlier strikes were indeed an expression of political discontent, rather than narrow labour market issues. The strikes therefore here are seen as pitting "us, i.e. the people" against "them, i.e. the political leadership." There are no signs of ethnic, racial or language-based separations of "us-them", but more of a citizen-based separation from leadership.

National community: political protests[58]

The political protests in France during the period June 1953 to March 1955 were mainly agricultural protests and violent demonstrations in Paris. I will focus on the agricultural and wine-producers' protests during 1953 on one hand, and on the most violent demonstrations and protests in Paris on the 14th of July, in March, April and August 1954 both in Paris and in the French Union, and also by the new Poujadist movement in January 1955.

In July the vineyard owners in four wine-producing departments in southern France demanded aid from the state, against the background of a declining market for wine and grapes. The government refused to purchase wine at a higher price, however. The result was a demonstration on the 28th of July 1953. Roads were blocked and municipalities closed. Only physicians and nurses were allowed to pass. In some parts, the protests did not end until the special force police (C.R.S) entered, while in other areas, support was less enthusiastic. For the government, negotiations were contingent on the end of the demonstration. The protests ceased, but the wine producers' intention was to enter into talks with the govern-

[58] Sources, if not anything else is mentioned, *L'Année Politique* 1953–1955.

3. FRANCE IN AN IDENTITY CRISIS?

ment, and stage a new demonstration on the 13th of August if negotiations proved unsatisfactory. In August, however, the major strikes began, and the wine-producers were not prepared to encourage new demonstrations at that time.

The agricultural workers' demonstrations were most prominent during the autumn of 1953, when farmers barricaded roads, protested locally outside district buildings and halted all agricultural production. The strike was effective in 14 districts, and was followed by additional demonstrations in the east of France. The government made efforts to meet the farmers' demands by curtailing the import of agricultural goods and increasing subsidies to farmers.

The political demonstrations were focused mainly on France's position in the French Union. On the 14th of July 1953, the traditional demonstrations of the Communist Party at Place de la Bastille led to disorder of about 2 000 individuals of North African descent; seven persons died and numerous more were injured as the police sought to impose order by force. The incident was discussed in the Assemblée Nationale, but demands that the government should recognize the political situation in North Africa were rejected.

In March 1954, the legitimacy of French possessions in India began to be questioned. India, independent since 1947, claimed sovereignty over Pondichéry, which had been a French holding in India since 1673. There were several violent clashes between French police and separatist elements that sought to formally separate Pondichéry from France and integrate the territory with India. There were also attempts to deliberately sabotage the customs regulation agreements between India and the French establishment. After several months of futile negotiation and intense political pressure from India (including the occupation of certain territories), the Assemblée Nationale decided on August 27th to engage in formal talks with India in the hope of safeguarding French interests. In October 1954 Pondichéry was transferred to India. The population was granted the right to choose its citizenship, but France retained the right to protect its citizens and preserve certain elements of their own education system in the area.

On the 31st of March 1954, the French Commander-in-Chief Maréchal Juin delivered a speech stating that the controversial Agreement on a European Defence Community (EDC) was technically "inapplicable" in its present form. Speaking of the government, Juin provocatively declared, "there is no longer a state, only an administration." On April 4, Prime Minister Laniel and Foreign Minister Pleven appeared at Place de l'Étoile to participate in the traditional ceremony at the Tomb of the Unknown

Soldier. They suddenly found themselves surrounded by a mob shouting "Down with Laniel" and "Hail Juin!" The crowd was so thick that the police was unable to come near the Prime Minister. It was with great difficulty that the two ministers were able to reach their cars. The event showed that the representatives of political power were viewed as symbols of betrayal – specifically in regards to the EDC, and that Maréchal Juin had popular discontent on his side.

When Tunisia received indications of possible autonomy, the people in the French protectorate of Morocco responded by demanding greater independence as well. France had earlier forced a change on the Moroccan throne, and many groups in Morocco demanded the return of the former sultan, Mohammad Bey Youssef. Bey Youssef was viewed as a nationalist, whereas his replacement, Mohammad Bey Arafa, was seen as more or less of a puppet. Those who demanded the restoration of Bey Youssef now also clamoured for new provisions on the autonomy of Morocco. Demonstrators and police clashed repeatedly in Morocco, culminating in a series of violent confrontations in August 1954. Europeans, as well as indigenous Jews and Moslems in Morocco alike were killed; at least 76 persons and many more were injured.

In January 1955 Pierre Poujade gathered several tens of thousands of shopkeepers and small businessmen in the Velodrome d'Hiver in Paris for a demonstration against the state's fiscal policies. Poujade demanded a tax-boycott. Because of Poujade's great popularity, the state identified the boycott as a genuine danger. There were also concerns regarding the magnitude of Poujade's movement, and its possible consequences in the National Assembly.

It is my contention that the rebellious practice discussed in this Chapter reflected confusion about national communities. There was conflict over territorial possessions, politics, and taxation, both in continental France and in the French Union.[59] When the farmers protested governmental policies, they were attempting to re-establish "old France," with its small farms, its goats and its cabbage patches. When the wine-producers requested that the government subsidize the wine industry, they were drawing on their image of France as a wine-exporter, and on some special connection between France and Bordeaux wine. When the military rose against political figures they did so out of the conviction that France could not be France without its army and its extra-European territories. But the people who lived in these territories and longed for independence had a

---

59 I have not discussed Algeria and Indochina because these issues are what is to be explained.

very different picture of France, a picture of France as a colonial power with oppressive traditions and confining rules.

The demonstrations and protests are thus interpreted here as a challenge to France as a national community. There was no clear categorization of who was a member and who was an outsider. Boundaries were drawn not only between territories, social classes and professional groups, but also between ethnic groups, indicating the existence of an identity crisis in French society. If the protests had been focused on a handful of political objectives, or had been limited to certain groups or territories, or restricted to a short period of time, it might have been difficult to argue that the protests reflected an identity crisis. But the facts, as described in this chapter, seem to confirm a full-fledged identity crisis.

National values: elections and polls[60]

Municipal elections were held in France in April 1953. I will briefly discuss the results, since they influenced the events of the summer and autumn of 1953.

In June 1953, municipal elections were held in Vietnam, and in October, there were elections to the Parliament of the French Union as well as regional elections in Vietnam.

I will also discuss an opinion poll from 1952, published in the English second edition of Philip Williams *Politics in post-war France* (1958).[61] Unfortunately, there are no more elections or published polls during my research period – June 1953 until March 1955.

I will review these events chronologically since they are seen here as indicators of a discourse that sought to define national values, a process that does not change suddenly, and that can be described as a sort of learning process.

There was no parliamentary election during my research period. In the 1951 election, the electorate gave the nascent Gaullist party just over 20 percent of its vote. In the parliamentary elections of 1956, the Poujadist movement, at the time a newcomer, obtained nearly 12 percent of the vote. After the 1951 election, three configurations for a majority government seemed possible: a national coalition government without the Communists (who obtained 26.5 percent of the votes), a Centre-Left coalition including the Socialists, and a Conservative coalition with the Gaullists. None of these scenarios materialized, however. A minority coali-

---

60   Sources, if not anything else is mentioned, *L'Année politique* 1953–1955
61   Williams 1958 p. 452 appendix VII.

tion government emerged instead under the leadership of René Pleven (UDSR), comprising the Independent Republicans (Centre-Conservative), the Radicals (Centre-Left), the MRP (Christian Democrats) and the UDSR (Centre). This coalition represented a minority of the voters, although the election system benefited small Centre parties at the expense of the Gaullists and the Communists.

The government fell after only a few months, and already in January 1952 a new coalition was formed under a new Prime Minister; Edgar Faure (Radical). This coalition proved short-lived as well. In March 1952, Antoine Pinay (Independent) formed a new government that survived for the remainder of the year. In January 1953 René Mayer (Radical) formed a new coalition, which also fell within four months. In June 1953 a new government was installed under Joseph Laniel after a 36-day crisis. Laniel represented the Independent group (moderate Conservative). In what was becoming an alarming pattern, this government also fell, this time after one year. It was at in the aftermath of the Laniel government that Pierre Mendès France, representing the Radicals (Centre-Left), was installed as Prime Minister. When his government also fell, in February 1955, Edgar Faure (also from the Radicals) became head of yet a new government.

In February and March 1952, during one of the government crises, *Institut Français d'Opinion Publique* (IFOP) conducted two opinion polls where the French voters could comment on the current political situation.[62]

For my purposes, it is interesting to explore issues that could be linked to national values. I have chosen to focus on the issues of ideology and worldview. IFOP has conducted their analysis on the basis of partisanship. The published results show a connection between voting behaviour and social-economic issues, as well as a connection between partisanship and ideological issues.

The demographic statistics show that most of the French voters (59 per cent) resided in small towns with populations of 20 000 or under. Nearly one-fourth of the voters describe themselves as peasants (23 per cent), and only 38 percent as employees, civil servants or workers. As much as 30 percent were house wives. These figures indicate a rural national environment in France with few modernising influences.

The general political context indicates a polarised society. Above all, there was a sharp divide between three groups: Communist voters, Gaullist voters and voters of other parties. Of the Communist voters, 50 percent

---

62 I do not know the number of interviews, but the figures are significant, according to IFOP. The 'don't know-answers' are omitted. I have not had the access to data.

supported revolution as the path to progress; among other voters, this figure was between only one and nine percent. Among Communists 40 percent wanted their party to forcefully seize power; 26 percent of Gaullists and only between one and 13 percent of other voters held this view. As much as 77 percent of Gaullist voters were in favour of prohibiting certain political parties and 55 per cent believed that the Communists were the greatest foes of parliamentary democracy. While other voters expressed similar sentiments, the figures are not nearly as extreme. Interestingly, 46 per cent of Communist voters maintained that the Gaullists were the greatest threat to parliamentary government (They also tended to be dissatisfied with current politicians, with only 12 percent believing that the government was made up of "honest men". Only 23 percent of Gaullist voters believed ministers to be "honest men.")

When asked about their world view, Communists, Gaullists and other voters again diverge sharply. For the Communists, the war in Indochina and the military were the most pressing concerns (46 percent). They tended to believe that rearmament increased the risk of war (83 percent), and feared that the presence of US troops in Europe also increased the chances of a new war (82 percent). Gaullist voters argued that political instability was the most urgent issue (62 percent), and tended to believe that rearmament would reduce the risk of war (60 percent) and that the presence of US troops either reduced the risk of war or made no difference (38 percent and 37 percent, respectively). On each of the questions, with the exception of the Gaullist stand on US troops, these are the highest levels. Among the Gaullist voters, who are nationalists, the perception of US troops is likely to mirror their ambivalence to the influence of the United States in France.

When asked to describe what drew them to their party, Communist voters emphasize the struggle against capitalism (39 percent) and the pursuit of peace (32 percent), while the Gaullist voters underlined the future of France (33 percent). No other questions among the other groups of voters resulted in such high scores.

We cannot, of course, draw definitive conclusions on the basis of a single opinion poll, but it does appear that the results are very clear on one point – that French society was divided and polarised over values. For the Gaullist voters (over 20 percent of the voters), France had a certain status linked to political stability and efficient military forces. For the Communists (over 25 percent), class struggle, disarmament and revolution were more important, as values, than the reconstruction of a strong national base. With these two camps as intense and resolute as they were in these years, and with both of them excluded from political power, society found itself virtually paralysed by this conflict. Both camps were unyielding on their perspectives, yet neither of them held any actual power.

A reform initiative that would create a National Assembly of Viet Nam was implemented in January 1953. Municipal elections were held on the 25th of January 1953, and regional elections in October. The third step in this process was to create a National Assembly. The principal aim was to grant Viet Nam a more democratic political structure and to provide the Saigon government with a base from which to administer the country. Unfortunately for the reform effort, only 1 900 of over 20 000 municipalities voted. The most important cities, however, including Hanoi, Saigon and Haiphong, did vote. The electoral register included all men over 21 years old who was registered in the census of 1951. From the French point of view, the Viet Minh used any and all means to sabotage the election, although no violence erupted.

Voter turnout in the election was fairly high – 80.2 percent – and higher in the centre than in the north and south of Viet Nam. In Saigon young nationalists and independent candidates obtained most of the votes, but in the Tonkin area, elected candidates campaigned on the protection of local interests. In Hanoi, on the other hand, a Leftist nationalist group in opposition to the Viet Minh gained all seats but one. France concluded that the election had been a success for the Vietnamese government headed by Nguyen Van Tam.

In October 1953 these municipal councils elected regional councils. The regional councils had a consultative role – as in France – where taxes, economic and industrial development and social issues in the region were in focus. Six hundred candidates were presented for six hundred mandates, so the election was more or less formal and there was not room for choice. The reform initiative essentially tried to export the French political system to the territories of the French Union, aiming at a future association between these territories and France.

As we saw earlier, French governments tended to survive no more than a few months, and in several elections the voters backed parties that had no direct influence on actual politics. In April 1953 the French voters elected mayors and local councils. In municipalities with populations of over 9 000, a proportional vote was used. The Communist obtained 28.8 percent of the votes, the Socialists 17.7 percent, and the Gaullists only 10.6 percent of the votes. Both the Republican Left and Christian Democrats received a greater number of votes than the Gaullist Party, indicating a resounding defeat for de Gaulle. In local politics, it was clear, the polarisation between the different political parties had tipped over to the advantage of the Communists. In light of this, it does not seem unreasonable to conclude that nationalist values – i.e. excluding values – had lost some of their appeal.

3. FRANCE IN AN IDENTITY CRISIS?

In October 1953 there was election to the Assembly of the French Union. Territorial councils outside of France elected half of the Assembly, and the French Parliament appointed the other half. In 1953, the half that was elected by Union territories was to be established. Most of the delegates were not re-elected, because local politics and personality played a more important role in these than in national elections. This did not, however, have a significant effect on the political composition of the Assembly. The French Union Assembly had 197 delegates, with the strongest political groups being the Gaullists (32 delegates), the Republican Left (30) and the Socialists (25). Most of the 14 political groups were very small, and some of them were groups with a territorial rather than an ideological character. The Assembly of the French Union was not an ideological hot spot, but rather a forum for discussion between the territories and France. The idea was to draw the territories into the political discourse that was prominent in the core – Continental France – and galvanise the Union on this basis.

Although I have found only weak indicators on the subject of national values, I would say that the reform initiative in Viet Nam and the French Union Assembly point to what I would call inclusive national values. The poll from 1952 indicates a polarisation between values that can be described as nationalistic and exclusionary and values that were of a more Republican,[63] and therefore inclusive, nature. The elections indicate a trend away from nationalistic and exclusionary values towards Republican and inclusive values. In this step of the analysis, no clear conclusion can be drawn about exclusionary or inclusive values. I will argue, however, that my material, although lacking, reveals a greater presence of inclusive than exclusionary values.

Conclusion

In the subject here under study, "us and them," or the *self-perception of the people*, – were characterized as "us – the people" against "them – the political leadership". There are no signs of ethnic, race or language-based separations of "us and them", rather a citizen-based separation of leadership and subjects. In defining the *national community* we see a questioning of France as a national community. It seems that the distinction between members and outsiders was nebulous. We find boundaries drawn between territories, classes and professional groups, as well as between ethnic groups. In discussing *national values,* I suggest that values tended toward

---

63 In France republican values are connected to secularisation, egalitarianism, citizenship and individualism, which are against nationalism that is connected to Catholicism, hierarchy, organic state and collectivism. See Demker 1993.

the inclusive, rather than exclusionary, although I concede that no definitive conclusion can be reached on the basis of the consulted material.

On the basis of the three analytical dimensions, the confusion of boundaries between members and outsiders and the polarisation of national values confirm the presence of an identity crisis in France during the period under study. Only in the realm of self-perception do we find a more clear conception, namely, that between "us – the people" and "them – the establishment." This could also be interpreted as a kind of identity crisis, although we then risk blurring the concept of identity with a vague conflict-concept. Because we have vague definitions of both national community and national values in the French discourse, I argue that an identity crisis figured also at the discourse level. The presence of an identity crisis on the discourse level in national French identity suggests that one necessary criterion for confirming an identity crisis has been fulfilled.

3.4 National Identity: Foundations

What, then, are the power relations that both limit and inform the possible arguments in the French national identity discourse? As stated earlier, the foundation of the national identity lies in political and parliamentary power relations. In my search for regulating rules, I will turn to particular individuals and political groupings that in their discussions and practice lead us to the foundations of this identity conception.

Two groups were particularly excluded during this period in French political life: the Gaullists and the Communists. The Communists were excluded from every government during the period, and no Gaullists were allowed in either, even under de Gaulle's leadership.[64] Alongside these two groups were what I call defectors and "out-criers". A defector is someone who departs from political life or the political apparatus due to some perceived conflict or ideological issue. De Gaulle and François Mitterrand were defectors. De Gaulle withdrew from his movement, the Rassemblement du Peuple Français (RFP) in May 1953, and Mitterrand left government in September over disagreements on French politics in North Africa. Pierre Poujade in his turn can be described as an "out-crier." Poujade gathered discontented people around him to protest the tax system. His followers tended to be shopkeepers and members of the lower middleclass who had grown tired of political instability and did not view the government as a source of legitimate political leadership. He was

---

64 In Laniel's government 28/6 1953 there were two ministers from former RPF.

achieved success in the election of 1956, but during my period Poujade was primarily a symbol for widespread discontent. A descendant of the French monarchy, the Comte de Paris Henri also was somewhat of an "out-crier." Although he did not lead a specific movement, the Comte's authority in conservative circles was significant.

Two issue-areas stand out more than others as hubs in the political debate:[65] the discussion on integrating in Europe, and the French constitution. As we saw in my earlier analysis of the media debate, the issue of a European Defence Community was highly sensitive, as were ongoing questions regarding the French constitution.[66]

The European Defence Community was brought up for discussion in the National Assembly in August 1954. The debate opened on the 25th of August and ended on the 31st. The National Assembly rejected the European Defence Community, but on the basis of procedural, rather than substantive, concerns. On August 30th, a "question préalable" was adopted by a vote of 319 to 264. A "question préalable" is an official statement noting that the National Assembly did not have sufficient time to deliberate the issue on the agenda. If a "question préalable" is adopted, the proposal that is under consideration is automatically rejected. This was the fate of the European Defence Community.

Adolphe Aumeran proposed a "question préalable" already before the debate had begun, and Edouard Herriot, a co-founder of the Radical Party, signed. Herriot therefore had the opportunity to give a speech advocating rejection, but a rejection that did not reveal the extent of the divisions within the Assemblée Nationale.

The government remained remarkably passive in the debate on the EDC. The Communist Party and the Gaullists voted against, as did half of the Socialists, half of the Republican Left and some of the Conservatives. Only the Christian Democrats (MRP) was whole-heartedly in favour of the EDC.

The circumstances surrounding the vote in the Assembly are interesting as well. Edouard Herriot had spoken against the EDC, and therefore also in favour of the adoption of a "question préalable." The Socialist Christian Pineau had tried to speak in favour of the EDC. For Pineau, the EDC was an opportunity for solidarity, while for the Radical Herriot, it reflected the amputation of French sovereignty. When the vote was announced, it was greeted with applause from the extreme Right, the Communists, and

---

65 Besides of course the colonial issue, which I do not discuss here.
66 For more empirical support of this standpoint see Kahler 1984, Demker 1993 and Aimaq 1996.

a number of Socialists and Conservatives. In all these camps, the deputies rose and sang the French national anthem, La Marseillaise. Many of the Centre deputies walked out. One of the Communists declared, "Today, the Communist vote counted!"[67], after which Communist deputies sang "The International," the Communist anthem.

In the midst of all this turmoil, several deputies made attempts to speak, initially at no avail. After a short while the President of the Assembly succeeded in restoring order. As we can see, the boundaries were drawn with ideological symbols, and the turmoil entailed some sense of solidarity between Communists and Gaullist, the two groups that were excluded from government. But this alliance was hardly a stable one, since directly following the election, the Communists and Gaullists diverged into a nationalist and an internationalist camp.

We may now identify outsiders and established individuals and groupings in the government formations from June 1953 to March 1954. In June 1953 Pierre Mendès France was rejected as Prime Minister. Joseph Laniel obtained the position, but not until after both Georges Bidault and André Marie had also been cast aside. Mendès France was a Radical. The Communist Party, more than half of the Gaullists and nearly the entire Conservative coalition, including nearly half of the Christian Democrats, voted against him. The Socialists supported him, however.

Georges Bidault was part of the M.R.P, the catholic Christian Democratic party, and was opposed by the Radicals, some Conservatives and many of the Gaullists and Communist Party. Both of these potential Prime Ministers were thus brought down by the Communist Party and the Gaullists, while the Radicals preferred Mendès France, and the Conservatives, Bidault. André Marie also tried to obtain the confidence of the National Assembly. As a Social Radical, Marie gained support from most of the Radicals, but not from the Christian Democrats or the Socialists. Marie thus was not supported by any of the more prominent groupings in the Assembly. When President Vincent Auriol finally selected Joseph Laniel, the crisis was in its 36th day. An Independent, Laniel was able to gather support among the Assembly's Social Conservatives. He received 398 votes, with 206 voting against him. Laniel had the backing of the Gaullists, the Radicals, the Christian Democrats and Conservatives, as well as his own Independents. Against him stood the Socialists and the Communists.

The crisis had thus led to a situation where the excluded groupings were the ones who effectively determined who the establishment would

67 Mopin 1988 p. 223.

be. The Communist Party, which held 102 seats in the Assembly (out of 627) and the Gaullists, with 120 seats, played key roles in deciding which of the other groupings would be in power. Yet the two groups, antagonistic to one another as they were, lacked the power to make themselves the establishment.

The next government crisis occurred in June 1954, when Pierre Mendès France was elected Prime Minister. The Communist group supported Mendès France, as did most of the former Gaullists. Only the Christian Democrats – (the M.R.P) – and a substantial part of the Conservatives abstained, with a minor number (47 MPs) voting against Mendès France. When Mendès France was overthrown in February 1955, the Communist Party had withdrawn its support. The Conservatives and Christian Democrats voted against him as well. All parties, with the exception of the Communist and the Socialist parties, supported the new Prime Minister George Bidault.

It is no exaggeration to say that the Communist Party and the Gaullist groupings played a central part in the power game of French governments in 1953–1955. Besides these two groups, Conservatives and Christian Democrats also played important roles, as did the Socialists. If we look at the government formations in 1953, 1954, and 1955, we find a constellation of powerful parliamentary groupings and more or less powerless individuals. Most of the ministers, and all of the Prime Ministers in this era, had held government posts already before the Second World War. Most of them were associated with particular issues or groups, although not necessarily with a particular parliamentary group at that exact time.

In sum, there were a few powerful groupings which supported some, out of very few, specific individuals on political grounds. And because these individuals lacked a clear association with any of the most powerful groupings, none of them felt a great obligation to be loyal or truthful on specific policy questions.

If we try and decipher what these grouping and individuals revealed about the French self-image, (in three dimensions, as discussed earlier) we find a Gaullist self-image, a Communist self-image, and also a contradiction between a Social Radical and a Social Conservative self-image.

The Gaullist Party, and after 1953 the excluded Gaullist group of U.R.A.S in the Assembly, promoted the self-image of a fragile and threatened France where international independence and imperial unity were a necessity for maintaining a national community.

The Communist Party, on the other hand, promoted a self-image where France was weakened from within, and where an economic revolution and the abandonment of the imperial concept where absolutely necessary.

They rejected all national communities other than the working classes. The struggle between the Social Radicals and the Conservatives focused on taxes and agrarian production, but also over colonial issues. For the Social Radical groupings, extended welfare systems, and economic reforms, including higher wages, were imperative. The national community as they perceived it could include colonies, though a more associative than dependent relationship. For the Social Conservative groupings, lower taxes and a state support for agrarian production were core issues, and their notion of a national French community included the territories in other parts of the world.[68] For the Communists and Gaullists, international issues were most important, while the Social Radicals and Social Conservatives were more focused on internal economic issues. And because these issues suffered the fate of replacing each other during these years, also the governments and their support were to succeed each other.

Conclusion

The foundation of national identity, namely, the dynamics of power relations, was thus a composite *self-perception* where "we" could be everything from the working class to a colonial imperial power; where the *national community* could include either "members" who were French only in the narrow geographic sense, or French in the broader cultural meaning; or where national community could be class-based with *national values* which can be described as inclusive. Given this assortment of various self-images, I would argue that also in the foundational level, France was gripped by an identity crisis at this time.

3.5 France in an identity crisis?

At this stage of the study, it seems undeniable that expressions of the French self-image during the period indicate that national identity was nebulous and ill defined. In short, France was in the midst of an identity crisis during the years 1953–1955.

We have seen that self-perception involves a "we" that is determined by history, geography, nation-state, class and empire. And this is the case on all three levels of the concept, namely, argument, discourse and foundation. We have also seen that the conception of *national community* varies,

---

68 These conclusions are based on both own earlier research (Demker 1993, Demker 1997, Demker 1998b) but also on secondary sources as the excellent studies Phillips 1958, Grosser 1961 and Aimaq 1996. For primary sources, see *l'Année Politique* 1953, 1954, 1955.

and might be founded alternatively on the political system, a value based community, territorial borders, professional groups or social classes. This also is the case on all three levels of the concept of identity. And we have seen that the conception of values is disputed far less on the argument level than on the discourse level. On all levels, French values are generally comprehended as universal, civic, and egalitarian. But it is not always the same substantive values that have these characteristics. Even though they are not all together the same, they are usually seen as something to agree on. On the foundational level, however, the values act as a differentiating factor, although they could also galvanise antagonistic groups, 'for the sake of France' or some similar sentiment.

From this part of the study, we now draw the conclusion that France was gripped by an identity crisis both before and during Mendès France's tenure as Prime Minister in 1954–1955.

4.
Pierre Mendès France as Part of the French Foreign Policy Elite

An individual cannot be isolated from his or her context. I have therefore chosen to approach Mendès France through an analysis of his "networks," where identity conflicts and his position in French foreign policy and within the political elite can be traced.[69] Network relations differ from hierarchy relations and market relations.[70] In a hierarchy, relations are formal, vertical and based on authority. Market relations are instrumental and are tied to gains and losses. In a network, however, all relations are horizontal as well as informal. An individual's position in the network is defined by his/her ability to control resources and by his/her social status. Being a part of a network entails a long-term engagement. Employing the "network" as a metaphor helps to focus research on long-term social patterns, social milieu, family connections and intellectual allegiances.

Maintaining a social network in reality requires mutuality, which can be attained through an exchange of favours, sharing sensitive information, or shared feelings of trust. We do not always wish to acknowledge that networks exist, or that they can be decisive to political outcomes. Many feel that networks are fundamentally illegitimate, irrational and suspicious. Highlighting their role, however, can help us structure our understanding of society in quite a different way than we normally do. Appreciating the existence of a network can help us understand a political outcome that could not be explained by a rational choice model. Negative images conjured up by the idea of a network might include the mafia, for instance,

---

69 Stenlås 1998.
70 Definitions from Stenlås 1998 p. 48 f. Also Carlsson 2000.

while a more positive image would be that of the agrarian family. The two images, however disparate, are two sides of the same coin.

I have chosen to discuss Pierre Mendès France from a network angle because of the power relations in the French elite at this time. I have opted not to focus on party politics, government coalition building or voting in the National Assembly. While these factors are certainly a part of the broader context, the main emphasis of my analysis lies elsewhere. As Joseph Nye has pointed out, power can also be "soft", and can be defined on the basis of ideological influence.[71] Certain parties may wish to emulate you, or otherwise please or satisfy you. In such cases, power is exercised without having to resort to direct pressure or violence. Power in – or through – a network is a form of soft power, not exercised via pressure or punishment but through favours, understanding and trust.

Many of the persons who were in the Cabinet or the National Assembly had close ties to one another, had been in the same political groupings, or had been struggling against one other since before the Second World War. Despite multiple shifts in governments and leadership during the period under study, there clearly existed a (Paris-based) political elite of which Pierre Mendès France was a part. His power, and the power which was exercised upon him, came through these political networks.

In this chapter, I will discuss Mendès France's background, and how it played in to creating his network. I will then describe and discuss his political network. The analysis will concentrate on his friends and foes, both inside and outside of his political alliance. The main focus of the analysis is the cleavage *between* Mendès France and his surroundings during the early 1950s. I will discuss identity conceptions in the foreign policy elite, aiming to reveal cleavages and different identity conceptions within this group. In the next chapter, I will deal with Mendès France's *own* conceptions while he was Prime Minister.

4.1 A conventional career?

Pierre Mendès France was of Jewish origin, both on his paternal and maternal side.[72] His Jewish background became an important factor as French anti-Semitism escalated. His lineage had historically been very patriotic, and the paternal side had even converted to Catholicism. His

---

71 Nye 1991. Power is conventionally seen as punishment, favoring or persuasion.
72 For references of the life of Pierre Mendes-France and his surroundings, Lacouture 1981, Leclerc 1984, Proust 1984, Mendès France 1992 and Stasse 2004.

father's family was from Bordeaux, his mother's from Sarrebourg. His parents were married in 1905 in Strasbourg, in Alsace, a French region that had long been disputed between France and Germany. Mendes-France was born in Paris in 1907, studied law, and at the age of 21 authored a dissertation about the fiscal policies of Raymond Poincaré. In 1932, Mendès France became the youngest French lawyer and the youngest deputy in the French Parliament. He represented the Radicals, and was primarily interested in economics. Already in 1930 he wrote a book about how an integrated Europe could develop its economic policy through an international bank. He also became Under-Secretary of State in the Treasury under the Leon Blum government in 1938. During the thirties, he met an older Left-Liberal journalist, George Boris, who he came to work with in the Treasury.

Before the war, Mendès France's career was quite conventional. Although he was very young for all of the positions he held, his career did not show signs of evolving into anything particularly noteworthy or original.

Mendès France married in 1933 and had two sons. He was first politically mobilized in 1939. A pivotal event took place in 1940. Mendès France was arrested for "desertion," although the true motivation for the arrest was his Jewish heritage. He was sentenced to six years in prison, but fled. He arrived in London in 1942 and joined the Resistance under Charles de Gaulle. His wife and children had escaped to the United States, and his parents to Switzerland. All of them survived the war.

Mendès France joined de Gaulle's shadow-government, and met General Catroux, the French governor for Indochina until 1939, in Algeria. General Catroux made a great impression on Mendès France and persuaded him that colonialism was not the future for any of the European states. Perhaps it was this meeting that launched Mendès France onto his new political path. Mendès France was also very much connected to the magazine *l'Express*, founded by Jean-Jacques Servan-Schreiber in 1953. *L'Express* was a political magazine with a radical slant that sought to initiate a more intellectual political debate in France. Colonial and economic policy was frequent topics in the magazine, as they were in many other new liberal journals, such as *l'Observateur/France-Observateur* and *Esprit*.

After the war Mendès France left de Gaulle's new government on the grounds of differing economic visions. His family returned to France in 1946, and the following year Mendès France became France's representative to ECOSOC (the Economic and Social Council of the United Nations). During his years with ECOSOC, Mendès France met several individuals – among them Gunnar Myrdal – who made him increasingly aware of the consequences of colonialism. He left ECOSOC in 1951. He had in the meantime also been a deputy in the National Assembly, and in 1950 he condemned French policy in Indochina openly in Assemblée Nationale for the first time.

He subsequently addressed the Assembly repeatedly, always admonishing the government of France on both economic and nationality issues. He argued that retaining Indochina was economically destabilizing and therefore a threat to French national pride. His suggestion was to initiate negotiations directly with the Vietnamese opposition camp, the Viet Minh. Such negotiations were considered impossible by French governments, all of which refused to negotiate, until the Laniel government finally succumbed in 1954. Before Laniel, each French government had tried to hold Indochina inside the French Union by force.[73]

Mendès France tried to obtain the confidence of the Assembly to form a government in June 1953, but failed. A year later he was asked again, and this time, he succeeded.

After his period as Prime Minister – which will be discussed further – Mendès France began to co-operate with the Socialists. He was Foreign Minister in the Guy Mollet government in the spring of 1956. Mendes-France also began a life-long relationship with a woman named Marie-Claire, who would become his second wife in 1971. He left the Radical Party, lost his seat in the National Assembly in 1958 and joined the new Partie Socialiste Unifié (PSU) in 1959. He was the PSU's candidate for Assemblé Nationale in 1962, 1967 and 1968, although he was defeated in each of these elections. His first wife, Lily, passed away in 1967. Mendès France suffered a heart attack in that year, and again in 1972. During the sixties, Mendès France supported Mitterrand's candidature in the presidential elections and remained staunchly opposed to de Gaulle's policies.

A close look at Pierre Mendès France's career reveals a man who never shied away from taking sides in conflicts. He used his leadership in political groups as a vehicle to promote the political values of his personal groups, rather than trying to influence the group itself. He only joined forces with individuals who shared his opinions – in a general sense – but what is most obvious is that he was not particularly focused on party loyalty or traditional political cleavages. His "entourage," or political brain-trust, during the years 1953–1956, can not be described as a traditional party-grouping, but more as a network of intellectuals strongly focused on colonial issues and the modernization and restructuring of France. They also shared an aversion to extreme nationalistic policies.

---

73 The war in Indochina led to nearly 100 000 dead and disappeared soldiers. Notes in Dossier Indochine III–IV, Institut Pierre Mendès France, Paris.

Mendès France's position was shaped by the shifting political landscape in France, changing from a clearly Liberal standpoint before the war, to a Liberal Socialist perspective during the 1960s. His position in the fifties was similar to that of a Nordic Social Democrat, but since there was no room for a genuine Social Democracy in France, he was forced to affiliate himself with various Liberal-Leftist groupings. It is important to note that the Gaullist movement exercised constant pressure in the French political arena from 1958 until the middle of the seventies, making it virtually impossible to be a Liberal without being on the Left. To present effective opposition during this period meant being a Leftist; no other position afforded any influence.

4.2   What was Pierre Mendès France's network?

In this study we focus on Pierre Mendès France as a decision-maker, and primarily a foreign policy decision maker. Mendès France did not have a single cabinet; he had at least three. First he had his Prime Minister cabinet, directed by André Pélabon, then he had his Foreign Ministry cabinet which was led by the diplomat Philippe Baudet, but where the de facto leader was George Boris, and third he had his "cabinet" at *L'Express* which was formed around Gabriel Ardant and Jean-Jacques Servan-Schreiber. In a way, Mendès France also had a fourth cabinet, namely, his team of negotiators during the Geneva conference, which included Jean Chauvel and Claude Cheysson as his principal advisers.[74]

In addition, Mendès France's second wife, Marie Claire Mendès France – born Schreiber – was an important source of both inspiration and political contacts. Marie-Claire and Pierre had a relationship that was both personal and professional. She was employed at *"L'Express"* during the 1950s, yet they did not marry until 1971. Mendès France remained betrothed to his first wife, Lily, until her death in 1967.

Marie-Claire was born to a family that was active in both politics and the media. Her mother was daughter to a senator, and her father was the founding owner of the journal *Les Echos*. Her cousin was Jean-Jacques Servan-Schreiber (JJSS), who, together with Marie-Claire and other members of the family, launched a weekly paper as a supplement to *Les Echos*. That supplement became *"L'Express"*, the journal that more than any other provided the space for Pierre Mendès France and his political perspectives.

Another important circle was the more or less informal group of

---

74   Lacouture 1981:231ff.

political advisors that surrounded Pierre Mendès France in his cabinet. The most prominent of these during our period was George Boris. Boris was the man with whom Mendès France discussed potential candidates for government and Boris was also the man who compiled the facts and figures that formed the basis for Mendès France's decisions. George Boris had a post as "conseiller d'Etat," but his role was both more personal and political than this title suggests. Boris was first of all the "eminence grise" behind Mendès France's government. He had known Pierre Mendès France since the middle of the 1930s. Boris and Mendès France worked together at the Treasury under the Blum government in 1938. Boris was a well-known journalist, twenty years older and more interested in international economics than Mendès France. Boris was initially a Socialist but became more of a Gaullist after the war. He was strongly influenced by Maynard Keynes and Franklin Delano Roosevelt in his economic views. Boris and Mendes-France also collaborated during the Résistance, and were both tied to de Gaulle during that time.

Boris was a sort of polyglot. Born in Lorraine to a family that owned a trading business, he travelled a great deal and was exposed to what he perceived as extensive human suffering. He became a government expert on economic negotiations after the First World War. Subsequently, he left France to work in Belgium, but returned as a journalist. He began at "Le Quotidien" in 1923 and founded "La Lumière," one of the most influential Left-wing newspapers during the late twenties and thirties, a few years later. It was through his position as a journalist that he first encountered Pierre Mendès France.

After the war Boris retained contact with exile-politicians from North Africa, and formed relationships with politicians and journalists with Liberal and anti-colonial leanings. Through Boris, Mendès France met people who had direct experience with French colonial policies. During his time at ECOSOC, he met people from other regions who likewise had anti-colonial sympathies.

André Pelabon was head of the Prime Minister's official cabinet and coordinated its operations. He was also part of Mendes-France's so called brain trust. After resigning in February 1955, Pierre Mendès France put up a shadow-cabinet and asked Pélabon to push harder on the sensitive question of Algeria. Pélabon had been responsible for intelligence and special police in the Resistance, and also had experience with Algeria as the delegate for Algerian affairs in the early post-war governments.

On colonial matters, Mendès France listened especially to René Lacharrière, Guy la Chambre, Jacques Soustelle, François Mitterrand (who was his minister for national issues), Jean Chauvel, Paul Martinet and Claude Cheysson.

Other important persons in Mendès France's environment were George Bourdat – with whom Pierre Mendès France exchanged letters until the 1970s – Jacques Legre and Pierre Soudet. These three also took care of his correspondence and archives. Pierre Mendès France was surrounded by Boris, Pélabon, Lacharriére, Bourdat and Martinet also in his ministerial cabinet in the spring 1956, alongside some new characters.

General Georges Catroux, whom Mendès France met in Algeria in 1943, may have been the first person to open Mendès France's eyes to the factual consequences of colonialism. Catroux had graduated from Saint Cyr in 1898 and went on to have a military career that took him to North Africa, the Middle East and Indochina. In June 1940, he rejected the armistice with the Germans and continued to support the Allies. He left Hanoi for London where he placed himself under the command of his junior, Charles de Gaulle. The General was tried in absentia and sentenced to death by the Vichy government in 1941. Catroux served as High Commissioner in Syria and Lebanon after Vichy forces were expelled. He became Governor of Algeria in 1943 and drafted laws designed to assimilate Algeria's Moslem population into full French nationality.

After the war Catroux became Ambassador to Moscow (1945–48), and after retiring he was recalled to become Governor-General of Algeria in February 1956. His announcement that he supported independence for certain French colonies triggered tremendous controversy, and after just four days in office, Catroux was forced to resign.

I have chosen to focus on the ideas, which grew out of the various foreign policy circles around Mendes-France, although I recognize that he was influenced politically from many different angles. However, since my research entails a discussion about identity as an explanatory factor in two cases of French de-colonisation, I believe that these circles are the most salient to the study. A very important fact to note is that most of Mendès France's confidantes had been affiliated with him already during the Résistance – as well as with de Gaulle – and that he had known many of them even before the war. During the 1950s a remarkably high number of them worked in the media and/or were journalists. Media was a very important arena for Pierre Mendès France.

4.3 Who were the opponents?

Although we could find individual persons whom we could call "opponents," it seems more relevant to note that those who opposed Pierre Mendès France were Conservative and Christian Democratic groups, many of whom wished to keep Algeria French. Wine producers and big business figured prominently among these groups. The military, which often felt a strong bond to the colonial empire, also opposed Mendès France's policy of autonomy and self-determination for many of the former colonies. Mendès France's most staunch opponents were not the men who were at the fore of the conservative groupings, however, such as Pinay, Laniel and Bidault. His most ardent opponents were among the men in his own party and in his own inner circles, and these men opposed him in large part because of his colonial policies. Edgar Faure, René Meyer and Léon Martinaud-Deplat of the Radical Party all opposed Mendès France's policies on Algeria. And his former friends Guy Mollet and Robert Lacoste both became adversaries after 1956, also over the Algeria question.

4.4 Which were the cleavages?

There is no doubt that the cleavage within the foreign policy elite concerned French identity. As we have seen in Chapter Three, France was in an identity crisis with several conceptions of France vying with one another. It would be unreasonable to contend that these cleavages would not be found among the foreign policy elite, when they could be found so readily among the population as a whole. Among the French population, identity conceptions were based on territorial, class and ethnic elements. I have also shown a cleavage in terms of "we – the people" and "they – the leadership". In the public debate I have shown the presence of historical, national, value-based and power-based cleavages. What, then, were the specific cleavages in the French foreign policy elite around Pierre Mendès France?

Identity, in this study, is a concept composed of three levels: arguments, discourse and foundation. As I have stated earlier, *foundation* is not subject to rapid change. *Arguments* represent the level at which change is most likely to be discernible. Change can occur at the discourse level as well, albeit quite slowly. I have here chosen to analyze certain men and certain actions among the elite with reference to cleavages in identity conceptions. First, we have Pierre Mendès France himself (1), then we have his network as mentioned earlier (2) and then we have his opponents both outside the Radical Party (Mollet, Lacoste, Pinay, Laniel) (3) and within the Radical Party (Faure, Mayer and Martinaud-Deplat) (4). I will look at the conception of France and the French Union in these four groups through the lenses of my earlier presented model. The material this time consists of internal papers, letters, telegrams, memoranda, manuscripts, speeches and personal notes. My interest lies mainly in uncovering the unofficial cleavages, cleavages that were not directly expressed in public, or expressed in public only later.[75] I have used material from Mendès-France's ministerial cabinets, compiled by his former colleagues. I have consulted neither official material nor material intended for a public audience. The first order of business for Mendès France was to have his views understood and accepted within his own network, and to respond to, and understand, the views of his opponents.

IDENTITY CONCEPTION	LEVELS OF EMPIRICAL ANALYSIS	WHERE TO FIND?
ARGUMENTS	Rhetoric content	Notes, letters, memos
DISCOURSE	Practice	Notes, letters, memos
FOUNDATION	Power relations	Decisions

Figure 4.1 Operative scheme and research material for analysing national identity at the individual level

I have chosen to analyze material that had a sort of policy-status (letters and memos) and material that appears as more of a commentary on statements (such as notes). Alongside these two categories, documents that reveal decisions made inside the cabinet (appointments, resignations, setting up workgroups) comprise a third category of material, helping to reconstitute the foundations of identity conception.

The same cleavages found among the population and reflected in the media debate are likely to exist also within the elite, but there is also a possibility of other, not officially recognized, cleavages in the elite. Besides searching for historical, ethnic, class or territorial identities, we therefore must be open to other, not foreseen identity cleavages. I argued earlier that self-image is a core part of national identity, and since this applies to elite conceptions as well, I have chosen to employ the same operative concept here. Because I must rely on a fairly limited material that is fragmented, selectively compiled, and geared internally, I have not found it necessary to evolve a content scheme to get a clear picture of the internal cleavages in the elite during Pierre Mendès France's time in government from 1954 to 1956. Instead I discuss each pattern in connection with the cleavages found.

---

75 All material for this analysis is at hand at Institut Pierre Mendès France.

4.5   Pierre Mendès France and the French self-image

As stated earlier, French self-image is here seen as composed of three issues. 1. What is France? 2. What sort of national community do we constitute? and 3. What are our national values? For Pierre Mendès France, France was mainly a European power, but there was room for a global role as well. He also believed that citizenship was by far more important than nationality. Pierre Mendes was an advocate of inter-state cooperation between France and the former colonies, rather than a federative or traditional colonial system. For some of the territories, such as Tunisia, he viewed independence as a viable option in the foreseeable future. He emphasized often that France had an obligation towards the less developed countries, but always highlighted national independence and autonomy as the models for these countries.

In a private interview, given in English for the John Foster Dulles Oral History Project at Princeton University, Pierre Mendès France said that autonomy for Tunisia "was considered as a scheme or a precedent which could be used later for other French governed territories. (...) I wanted to pursue an emancipation policy in Algeria".[76]

In a written note to Pélabon on the 20th of October 1956, Mendès France emphasized that France, Morocco and Tunisia shared common interests which could only be pursued through joint efforts, although France would always have "le poids décisif", or the final say, "if we are intelligent," as he would say.[77] It is obvious that Mendès France viewed France as a territorial state separate from both Morocco and Tunisia, but he nevertheless made remarks that suggest a certain sense of colonial responsibility. In an internal discussion in the Radical Party in April 1957, Mendès France also referred to the incompatibility between the war in Algeria and French civilization when he condemned the use of torture by the French military in Algeria.[78]

In the preparations for his speech before the Executive Committee of the Parti Radical of April 20th, 1956, Mendès France made an interesting edit. The original manuscript referred to "notre pays" (our country), but Mendès France personally crossed this out and replaced it with "le pays" (the country). Later, an internal debate took place with Mendès France refusing to accept the words "l'intégrité de l'Algérie Française" in a Radical

---

76   Dossier V (1) Indochine Transcript of interview made by Dr Philip A. Crowl 17/6 1964.
77   Dossier Pierre Mendès France vol Cabinet II 20/10 1956 PMF à Pëlabon.
78   Dossier Legré vol 4 10/4 1957 protocole.

Party declaration on Algeria. He insisted that the phrase "l'integrité de l'Algerie" be used instead.[79]

Mendès France had made a similar edit in a manuscript for a National Assembly speech many years before, on the 19th of October 1950, where he replaced "l'échelon national" (national scale) with "l'échelon mondial" (international scale) in reference to the Indochina War.[80]

Mendès France appears to have viewed France as a territorial unit with a primarily European base, but with obligations towards former French governed territories. These obligations, however, are seen as part of the international context. This was illustrated in January 1955, for instance, when he wrote to Guy de la Chambre, Minister of The French Union, to complain about the South Vietnamese government under Ngo Dinh Diem. In his letter, Mendès France argued that the Geneva Accords bound France to grant total independence to Vietnam, and that France was to follow through on this commitment, although the Diem government was "peu compréhensif à notre endroit" ("not particularly understanding of our position"). If the government did not alter its course and implement the Geneva Accord, Mendès France argued, a change in government would be "souhaitable" (desirable).[81] We thus see that even in his private correspondence, Mendès France insisted that adhering to the international agreement was more important than trying to change internal Vietnamese policy.

In the wake of the Geneva Accords of July 20th 1954, Mendès France foresaw the possibility of a great influx of refugees into France. He also feared that the free elections stipulated for 1956 would bring to power a Communist regime in the whole of Vietnam, which would generate an even greater refugee flow, mainly among French citizens living in the area. In reality, most of the French refugees crossed the demarcation line from North to South Vietnam, and many French citizens also moved to other French territories. In a memo to Guy de la Chambre, shortly after the Geneva Accords, Mendès France warned that there would be "parmi les Français et les Euroasien de citoyenneté Française désireux de quitter la zone qui va passer sous le contrôle de la République Démocratique de Vietnam" (among the French and the Eurasians of French citizenship those who would like to leave the zone controlled by the Democratic Republic of Vietnam –[the Viet Minh]). Interestingly, Mendès France

---

79 Dossier Pierre Mendès France vol Afrique du Nord/Gouvernment Guy Mollet 20/4 1956 manuscript.
80 Dossier Indochine vol I 19/10 1950 manuscript.
81 Dossier Indochine vol V (2) Note to Guy la Chambre 4/1 1955.

suggests that France help these citizens move to other French territories, which they could then help develop, such New Caledonia, Madagascar and Guyana. These migrating French citizens, he argued, would enhance the influence of France in these territories, and "ne féront pas cause commune avec les autochtones" (would not ally with the indigenous peoples).[82] He clearly distinguished between French influence and French citizenship. The note illustrates the dilemma between national power and national community. There is no doubt that Mendès France understood citizenship as the principal basis of national community, but he also exhibited a certain inclination in favour of French power politics in the overseas territories. It is evident that he did not view territories such as New Caledonia and Madagascar as candidates for independence as he did Vietnam, Morocco, Tunisia and perhaps Algeria.

Mendès France seems to have perceived France as a European territory but also as a civilization with external obligations, an identity that thus is both territory- and value-based. Membership in the national community rests on citizenship. Mendès France's national values reveal an apparent dichotomy regarding French global power politics, and commitments to international treaties, and national independence and autonomy. I believe that this dichotomy was informed by Mendès France belief that if the territories were, or contained, a national community – (in the French sense) they should be granted independence. If not, they should be governed by the French authority. The right of a national community to govern itself is therefore a fundamental value for Mendès France.

4.6 Mendès France's network and French self-image

One of Mendès France's closest collaborators, Renè de Lacharrière, wrote to him in April 1956, just after Mendès France has decided to leave the government, requesting that he pose a final question to Guy Mollet.[83] A government writes Lacharrière, that is a French Republican government, cannot conduct a war of repression in Algeria, a war that is widely viewed as "colonialiste". If the Socialists, who are the head of government, do not acquiesce to immediate measures, such as freeing political prisoners, censor of the colonialist press, expropriate big estates in Algeria the responsibility would be entirely theirs. If they agreed to implement these measures, so much the better.

---

82 Dossier Indochine vol V (2) Note to Guy de la Chanbre 25/9 1954.
83 The letter is found in Dossier Pierre Mendès France vol Cabinet I.

There is no doubt that Lacharrière felt that France was, or should be, the power in charge in Algeria. Nor is there any doubt that Lacharrière put French Liberal opinion in Europe first. It is its security and its values that he primarily sought to promote. George Boris also emphasized that French opinion believed Frenchmen in Europe wished to negotiate with "les musulmans".[84] But in a memorandum just preceding Mendès France's resignation, Boris also notes that the security of the "Français d'origine européenne" in Algeria must be ensured before any negotiations. Boris thus viewed France as a territorial power and the Frenchmen in Algeria as Frenchmen by descent. This view was echoed in a statement by Pierre Soudet, another member of Mendès France's entourage, who wrote that every proposal for Algeria must be discussed in the light of the need for suzerainty for "la personnalité algeriènne".[85] (Soudet cooperated with François Mitterrand in drafting proposed reforms for Algeria in 1955.)

Pélabon, who alongside Boris appears to have been Mendès France's most intimate collaborator, likewise spoke of two populations in Algeria, one French and one Algerian (or "musulmane," as the indigenous Algerian population often was referred to). Pélabon wished to improve the capabilities of the Algerian population through "formations professionelles," i.e. that French enterprise should provide education to French workers in Algeria. After that, says Pélabon, the Algerian people "fourniraient, une fois formés, une excellente main-d'oeuvre qualifiée pour les entreprises métropolitaines" (provide, once educated, the French firms in Europe with an excellent and qualified labour force.).[86] There is no doubt that several of the members of Mendès France's cabinet did not explicitly share his view of France as both a territorial unit and a civilization, and of a national community grounded on citizenship. None of them discussed the "musulmans" in citizenship terms, and most of them believed that France was in Algeria as a separate nation-state, and not that these two territories constituted a single national community.[87]

The values held by members of Mendès France's entourage are very much concealed, since their role was first and most to serve Mendès France's values. Nevertheless, the edits in the manuscripts discussed above, and the manner in which Pélabon and Boris treat Algeria as a territory with two distinct populations, indicate that Pélabon and Boris held a more

84 Dossier Cabinet vol I PM.
85 Dossier Sou vol IV PM.
86 Dossier Algerie vol III 5/1 1955 Letter from Pélabon to Bourdat.
87 There is a long discussion between Pélabon and Bourdat about citizenship in Algeria about election laws in January 1956, but that very interesting discussion – which we will return to in a following chapter – was initiated by Mendès France himself.

nationalistic self-image than did Mendès France. I would say, after going through all the memoranda, notes and letters from the group behind Mendès France that it was he alone who introduced a new political concept.

4.7 Opponents outside the Radical Party: Guy Mollet, Robert Lacoste, Antoine Pinay and Joseph Laniel

It is obvious, even after a cursory analysis, that Mendès France's notions of the French Union were quite different from those of, for example, Pierre Poujade, a right-wing extremist, or those of many of the nationalists in Algeria who wrote the most appalling anti-Semitic letters to Mendès France.[88] But given my focus on networks, power and discourse, it is more interesting to characterize the opposition that came from the within the group that directed French foreign policy.

Guy Mollet, who became Prime Minister after the elections of January 1956, was the head of the Socialist Party (SFIO). He and Mendès France had formed an electoral coalition in the 1956 elections, and had decided to form a government that would include both of them and both of their parties. But once Mollet was offered and accepted the post of Prime Minister, the Algerian issue came under his authority. Algeria had never had a specially designated minister, which could be interpreted as another indication that Algeria was considered an integral part of France and could therefore not be treated as a separate issue. Contrary to earlier policy, Mollet established a specific department for Algeria, and asked General Catroux to assume control of it. It is self-evident that Mendès France felt excluded from this process.[89] The spring of 1956 witnessed a veritable tug-of-war on the Algerian issue between Mollet and Mendès France, which ended with Mendès France's resignation in May 1956.

A visit to Algeria in January 1956 proved pivotal to determining Mollet's policy on Algeria. Upon his return, Mollet delivered a speech to the Assemblée Nationale on the 16th of February 1956. A main theme in the speech was that the Europeans in Algeria felt abandoned by France. It seems that during his journey, Mollet had come to the conclusion that the Europeans in Algeria were much more like Frenchmen in France than

---

88 In the PMF-archive there are several personal letters from citizens that make references between Mendès France being a Jew and his "betrayal" of France by first giving Indochina away, and now trying to do the same with Algeria.

89 PM from 1956 by PMF, not dated, Dossier Pierre Mendès France vol Afrique du Nord/ Gouvernement/Guy Mollet.

like indigenous Algerians. In his speech Mollet distinguishes exclusively between "les Européens" and "les musulmans", "la collectivité musulmane" or "les populations musulmanes".[90] These concepts exclude the possibility of a common Algerian population, but include some of those who live in Algeria within the French community. It is interesting to note that in his speeches, Mendès France employed the concept "la population Algerienne"[91], a concept that includes everyone in Algeria, but excludes the idea of a common population in Algeria and France.

Mollet spoke of "la France" that had "traversé" ("passed through") the Algeria of the Europeans. He emphasized that the Europeans in Algeria could not possibly live elsewhere than in their homeland, Algeria, and because of this "la France" had an obligation to protect the "indissoluble" union with Algeria.[92]

In a radio speech on the 28th of February 1956, Mollet chose to emphasize that France, as a "loyale et généreuse" (loyal and generous) nation would offer both justice and equality to the Algerians. France would mobilize all of its efforts to ensure the security of the population of Algeria.[93] We can observe that Mollet makes a distinction between France and Algeria. France is a community with resources, and will provide as a generous gift justice, equality and security to an Algeria in great need of these values. France is then associated with Republican values (justice and equality) and with power resources (security) while Algeria is associated with the lack of these values.

Mollet, who has been held responsible for the escalation of the Algerian War because of his massive deployment of re-enforcement troops, held the belief that France was a both territorial unit and a value-based concept. Here we have the same confusion that was reflected in the media debate (Chapter Three). But Mollet also retained the idea that France was associated with the power-resources, which could guarantee the values in which he placed such great stock. We must conclude that Mollet's France was a France of great power and influence.

For Mollet the French community was defined not by citizenship, but by ancestry. The population of European ancestry in Algeria was included in Mollet's idea of a French community, while the others were not. National community for him could therefore be said to be histori-

---

90   Speech of Mollet 16/2 1956, Dossier Algerie vol VIII.
91   Speech at Parti Radical's executive committee 20/4 1956, Dossier Pierre Mendès France vol Afrique du Nord/Gouvernement/Guy Mollet.
92   Speech of Mollet 16/2 1956, Dossier Algerie vol VIII.
93   Speech note Mollet 28/2 1956, Dossier Algerie vol VIII.

cally defined. Mollet was a Socialist, and the values he held were universal values such as equality and justice. But for Mollet there was also a class based universe where Europeans in Algeria, many of them with a working class identity, should enjoy the same conditions as the working class in metropolitan France.[94] For Mollet, national values therefore came to differentiate between groups in the same territory. For him, the "musulmans" were not included in the French working class and he either lacked the sensitivity – or mindfulness – to understand that equality also has a global side, namely international solidarity.

Robert Lacoste, one of Mendès France's friends, was made Governor-General of Algeria in February 1955 by Mendès France just before he had to resign as prime minister. When he took possession of that post, Lacoste shared Mendès France's view that Algeria should not be a re-play of Indochina.[95]

Already by April 1956, some of Lacoste's views had shifted. In his speeches from that month, Lacoste appears convinced that the bonds between France and Algeria must be maintained and that the rights of the Europeans in Algeria should be protected.[96] In a report to the French government on the 12th of December 1956, Lacoste writes that it was France that had created Algeria as well as "le sentiment d'une collectivité algérienne propre" ("the sense of a genuine Algerian community"). Lacoste thus denies the existence of a pre-French Algerian national community. He excludes the possibility of an Algeria without or before the France presence.[97] Later, in April 1957, Lacoste denied the entry into Algeria of a French investigation committee from the Radical Party.[98]

On Algeria, Robert Lacoste came to share the views of Prime Minister Guy Mollet. During his tenure in Algeria, Lacoste increasingly acted as the representative of the Europeans in Algeria to the Paris government, rather than vice versa. There are no traces of Lacoste's own visions for Algeria in the archival material, but an overview of his official statements indicates that he advocated a future where France still enjoyed supremacy in Algeria, although not as a repressive force. Judging from Mendès France's critique of Lacoste, the Governor-General found himself lacking the resources

---

94 The Socialist party had its bastions of support among middle aged civil servants who was not interested in a social process of change. Berman 2006:194.
95 Lacoste i Combat 24–25/3 1956 Dossier Pierre Mendès France vol Afrique du Nord/ Gouvernement Guy Mollet.
96 Lacoste's speeches, Dossier Soudet vol 5.
97 Lacoste-report 12/12 1956 Dossier Soudet vol 5.
98 Letter from Lacoste 24/4 1957, Dossier Legré vol 4.

necessary to both conduct reforms and fight terror in Algeria.[99] He chose to commit the resources he did have to the struggle against the Front de Liberation National (FLN), thinking that when the 'terrorists' were beaten; there would be time for reforms. Lacoste's France was a great power, a territorial unit, and France had the duty to mitigate the situation in Algeria, while reforming the territory both socially and economically. For Lacoste, Algeria and France were associated with each other through historic destiny.

Antoine Pinay, a market Liberal, and Joseph Laniel, a Liberal Conservative, both independent deputies in the Assemblée Nationale and Prime Ministers before Mendès France, were among his most important critics. They were both over fifteen years older than Mendès France. Pinay had voted for Pétain in 1940, but helped the Resistance during the war. Pinay was interested in economic policy and was a market Liberal, yet was strongly attached to the idea of a French Algeria. Despite this, he helped pave the way for autonomy in Tunisia, a project that was brought to fruition by Mendès France. Joseph Laniel lost the Prime Minister post over the fruitless negotiations in Geneva on Indochina in 1954, and was directly succeeded by Mendès France. Laniel and Pinay opposed Mendès France on two major foreign policy issues, Indochina and Algeria. Laniel, together with his excellent negotiator George Bidault, discussed possible solutions for Indochina. Although none of them could accept the division of Vietnam, Pinay, Bidault and Laniel appeared to make intermittent progress on the question. Pinay had initiated negotiations between France and Tunisia for potential autonomy, and also participated in the discussion to grant Morocco an autonomic status within the French Union. None of these men belonged to the colonialist lobby that categorically opposed all independence or autonomy for the colonies.

In a debate in the Assemblée Nationale in May 1956, Pinay and Laniel stood out as two of the most prominent critics of French policy in Algeria. They denounced the abandonment of the Europeans in Algeria and drew parallels to the "sacrifice" made in Indochina.[100] Laniel had been politically forced to favour a solution through negotiation in Indochina just prior to his resignation. And Mendès France had not waited long to take advantage of Laniel's policy shift to put forward his own plan for negotiation directly with Ho Chi Minh.

Antoine Pinay seemed quite tolerant of Mendès France's positions, until it was revealed that Mendès France's views on the Algerian issue clearly

---

99   Letter from PMF to Lacoste 5/4 1956, Dossier Pierre Mendès France vol Afrique du Nord/Gouvernement Guy Mollet.
100 "Le temps du Paris" 26/5 1956, Dossier Bourdat vol 2.

did not entail "an Algérie Française." Pinay was among those who tried to form a government after Mendès France's resignation in February 1955. Pinay and Laniel represented the opposition to Mendès France outside of his own party coalition, but this was not tantamount to a hard right-wing colonialist position. It was the critique from these Center-Liberal politicians – to whom a French Algeria was a matter of the heart – which points to a cleavage inside even the relatively liberal foreign policy elite.

Inside the foreign policy elite, territory-based conceptions of the French self-image dominated, although a history-based French self-image also figured. This was in contrast to Mendès France's territorial but value-based self-image. This cleavage, which was outside the party but inside the foreign policy elite, demonstrates clearly that the self-image with self-perceptions of France, national community and values were not undisputed even among the small group that held power over foreign policy during these few years.

4.8 Opponents within the Radical Party: Edgar Faure, René Mayer and Léon Martinaud-Deplat

The Parti Radical (PR) was established in 1901, mostly as a reaction to the influence of the French Catholic Church. From the start, the party included a Left and a Right wing. During the 1930s, the Radicals became more and more of an electoral machine to bring up candidates in the elections. Pierre Mendès France, who became a deputy in 1932, belonged to a group called "the Young Turks" that was associated with renewal and Leftist leanings. During the Fourth Republic the Radicals had between 10–15 percent of the electoral vote. Mendès France increased the level of support among both the working classes and the Left-leaning Catholics.[101] But when he had left his post as Prime Minister the Radicals split between the Mendesists and a Right-wing faction led by Edgar Faure. Faure had been Minister of Finance and also of Foreign Affairs in Mendès France's government, and took over as Prime Minister after Mendès France in February 1955.

At the Radical Party congress in November 1955, Mendès France assumed the leadership of the party, in practice, if not officially. His program was voted in as the electoral platform and he became First Vice President of the party. Faure was already the president of a loose coalition of Leftist Radical groupings outside the Socialist camp – the Rassemblement de Gauches Républicaines (RGR) – and tried to use this position to form a Radical

---

101 Larkin 1997:239.

electoral alternative without Mendès France. But the result was that Faure was ousted from the Radicals in December 1955. Mendès France joined an alliance of Leftist Radicals with Guy Mollet and the Socialist Party in the elections in January 1956, and Faure joined up with Conservative and Catholic groups. After the election Mollet was appointed Prime Minister.

Faure's criticisms of Mendès France were mainly party strategic. Faure wanted to make the Radical Party more cohesive, but on Centrist grounds, than Mendès France wanted. And the group around Mendès France viewed Faure's precipitation of the elections of 1956 (from June to January) as an attempt to frustrate Mendès France's plan to renew the Party. During the course of 1955, Faure's government lost control over events in Algeria, providing Mendès France's with his main line of criticism against Faure.

Faure did not appear particularly interested in resisting the nationalist sentiments in the Radical Party, on either side of the Mediterranean that still clamoured for a French Algeria. Faure seems not to have understood that the issue of a French or independent Algeria was far more complicated than simply liking or disliking the Algerie Française-lobby inside the party. Pélabon writes that Faure, then still Prime Minister, had said, at an official lunch with security counsellors in Algeria, that the Algerian issue now (Jan 1956) is "mûre" ("ripe") and could be settled within three months.[102]

The most prominent spokesman for the Algerie Française-lobby inside the Radical Party was René Mayer. He was a deputy for the city of Constantine in Algeria, a former Prime Minister, and was the man whose speech turned the majority in the National Assembly against Mendès France when he was resigning on the 5th of February 1955. Mayer and Léon Martinaut-Déplat had been opposed to Mendès France's North Africa-policy since the start. Martinaut-Déplat had also been the alternative candidate to Mendès France for the post of Administrative President of the Party, at the Radical Party congress in October 1954. Martinaut-Déplat was the one who won, with 746 votes to 689. Subsequent rumours about forged election cards were suppressed.[103]

In his speech Mayer said that "Français musulmans" (French Muslims, or 'Arabs') had been betrayed by the French policy. He also drew parallels to Indochina, and noted that adapting to the "monde moderne" always seemed to require "adapting" to the Arab nationalists or to anti-French groups. Mayer argued that France had to demonstrate that the government was "intransigeante" (intransigent) on anything that could sever

---

102 Letter Pélabon to Mendès France 10/1 1956, Dossier Bourdat vol 3.
103 *L'Année politique* 1954:82.

"des Français d'origine européenne" (Frenchmen of European ancestry) from France.[104]

In his speech, Mayer thus distinguished between Frenchmen of European ancestry and Algerians (musulmans) who held French citizenship or/and a French cultural identity. On one hand, Mayer's conception of French community included everyone of European descent, to the exclusion of all others. On the other hand, others could also be part of the French community through citizenship and/or affinity with French values. And in neither of these cases should metropolitan France – a territorial unit – abandon them. Only one group was therefore defined and excluded: those who lived in Algeria but were not of European ancestry and did not feel an affinity with French values. Mayer's position implied that for people of European descent, there was no identity conflict; but other persons living in Algeria had to make an identity choice.

For Mayer, as for most of the Algerie Française-lobby, Algeria was a territory, but not a unit. It was made up of populations, not of one population. It was created out of French values and belonged to the French community by these historical ties. Those who sought to separate the two territories, and who viewed Algeria as a discrete unit, had betrayed French values and France itself. In Mayer's eyes Mendès France was one of these traitors.

Faure in one corner and Mayer and Martinaud-Déplat in the other represented the two most powerful groups of internal critics of Mendès France. Edgar Faure was a Liberal-Centrist politician with vast experience with government cabinets and the Assembly. He believed that Mendès France worked too quickly and had overly Leftist leanings. Faure wanted to form governments in the centre and thereby to bring the Radical Party in influential positions.

Mayer and Martinaud-Déplat represent the Radical Party's provincial stronghold against Mendès France's Paris-based intellectual think-tanks. Algeria was a cornerstone in Mayer's and Martinaud-Déplat's conceptions of France. For them, Algeria had no identity of its own, and the people there were either "French" or "musulmans", depending on ancestry, but never "Algerian." And because of that conception, they, and the Algerie Française-lobby, could not accept a Prime Minister intent on holding the door open for autonomy. In their world that door had to be shut.

---

104 *L'Année politique* 1955:190.

4.9 Conclusion

Pierre Mendès France had an intellectual network that consisted of several groups of persons who were, more or less, experts in their field. On international political matters, George Boris and André Pélabon enjoyed a privileged position. It is clear from the archival material that the views and reactions of Mendès France tended to be thoroughly discussed by one, or several, of the small groups. Yet it is also clear, after a careful review of the personal documentation, that Mendès France himself was the driving force in these discussions. Boris appears to have been the only one who at times made comments that were not initiated by Mendès France. Judging by the notes and letters in the archives, Mendès France used his network to evolve arguments and to investigate issues – a process that left him free to make political choices on a remarkably independent and intellectual basis. He seems not to have been personally dependent on anyone, with the exception of Boris, and this also rendered him largely independent of his own network.

The network itself was marked by cleavages. Some among Mendès France's inner circles did not share Mendes-France's perspectives on the North African issue. A number of notes written by his closest collaborators indicate that France, while territorially defined, would not be "France" without Algeria. Likewise, Algeria is not always seen as a territorial unit of its own. Within Mendès France's network, the image of the population in Algeria at times at times distinguished between a "European" and a "Muslim" population. The French national community was thereby understood as comprising French citizens in metropolitan France adding the Europeans in Algeria, while the "musulmans" in Algeria are excluded – but therefore not despised.

There is a common emphasis within the network on social equality and national self-determination as national values. Therefore, all proposals aim at a solution that would be acceptable to everyone in Algeria and that would preserve Algeria as a mixed society with its own "personality". On the Indochina issue, by contrast, there is not a trace of cleavages inside the network.

The criticism from outside the network focused mainly on Algeria, and exhibited a split between conceptions of Algeria as a community with its own right to autonomy, within or without the French Union, and conceptions of Algeria as an integral part of France. Viewing Algeria as an integral part of France, Mollet argued for both equality and justice in that territory. For the outside critics, Mendès France's view of Algeria as a national community that could not be guaranteed these values by another nation was alien. For Mollet and Lacoste, France had an obligation towards Algeria because of the Europeans residing there, while for Pinay and Laniel, opposition to Mendès France's ideas was based on their conception of a territory-based national identity. And for the colonialist lobby, Mendès France appeared to be advocating a betrayal of national pride and history. For this group, Algeria had been invented and shaped by France, and could not simply be abandoned, as could other colonies.

The critique from within the network focused not only on Algeria, however, but also on the position of the Radical Party in the French political system. The party had long-standing ties with the provincial and traditional middle-class bourgeoisie. Some of these groups did not support Mendès France's foreign policy, which they found too adventurous. Some of them also had tight connections to – or were – wine producers or farmers in Algeria. There was not so much room within the party for an ideological renewal on the basis of national self-determination and market-economics. Mendès France's ideas on the improvement of France's economic power through the settlement of the colonial empire were not accepted in the Radical Party. The Radical Party has earlier not been known to be the kind ideological platform that Mendès Frances used it for. There were many influential persons, such as Faure, who felt a strong affinity for the old caucus organization where the deputies had influence on policy through membership, or support of, on centre governments.

An important conclusion in this study is that not even in the foreign policy elite was there a consensus about the French national self-image. Conceptions of France varied, as did conceptions of the national community. There was greater agreement on national values. Arguments centred on differing views on how to define the French national community, and on what obligations France had toward the rest of the world. The discourse could not transcend territorial definitions and problems of territorial descent. The foundation of the identity discussions concerning decolonisation in the foreign policy elite was the absence of true power in the political system. This void made military assessments decisive to political decisions, and also created the space for forceful lobbying from economic interest groups and extremists.

Because there were so many different conceptions of France, even within the narrow foreign policy elite, it was much harder to gain support for a political position that did not demonstrate a clear conception of national identity as its basis. Mendès France could have legitimated one or another of these conceptions, but he did not. The reason is that he chose to argue for an intellectual position, which means that he did not first define the goal and then draft the strategy. Inside the foreign policy elite, Mendès France advocated for a decolonisation that was grounded in national values such as equality and justice, but with great openness for alternative goals. But it simply was not possible during this time to argue over colonial issues without having a clear, identity based, goal for policy. You were either categorically for or against the French empire. Mendès France was neither. For this reason, he found himself isolated.

5.
Pierre Mendès France and the Conception of France

Pierre Mendès France did not have the same conception of France, or the same conception of the colonial empire, as most other members of his network. As discussed in Chapter Four, neither his adversaries nor his friends shared his value-based conception of France or his wishes for negotiable solutions that were not polarised between imperial or not-imperial goals. What, then, were Mendès France's conceptions of France?

5.1   What is a conception of France?

As argued in Chapters One and Two, a particular conception of national identity is important since it lays the groundwork for foreign policy decision-making and for the possibility of introducing, and receiving acceptance for, new approaches in foreign policy. Most foreign policy research focuses on why things happen when they do, rather than on the fact that they happen at all. I argue that a specific national identity conception prevented France from changing its colonial policy after 1954, despite the fact that Mendès France had solved the Indochina crisis. The explanation for France not being able to alter its policy lies in the conflicting conceptions of national identity that existed at the time. The conception of France is therefore key to understanding why a foreign policy change in the colonial context did not come about.

In previous chapters I discussed how to analyze national identity conceptions on the aggregate level and in foreign policy networks. This chapter presents an analysis of a distinct conception as expressed by a specific individual. In one sense, this analysis is far simpler, since the context is narrowly defined. Yet it also poses a significant challenge, since one person can play different roles at different stages, and my analysis could therefore reveal several different conceptions. As an analytical tool for my analysis, I shall rely on the scheme – slightly adjusted – from earlier chapters. Adjustments have been done to catch the same content as in earlier chapters, but now from a material that is produced by one man. Here it is impossible to follow arguments in a debate, I do not discuss his political practice and his power resources as prime minister or minister. Instead I try to dig deeper in his own language, his own arguments and is own reflections.

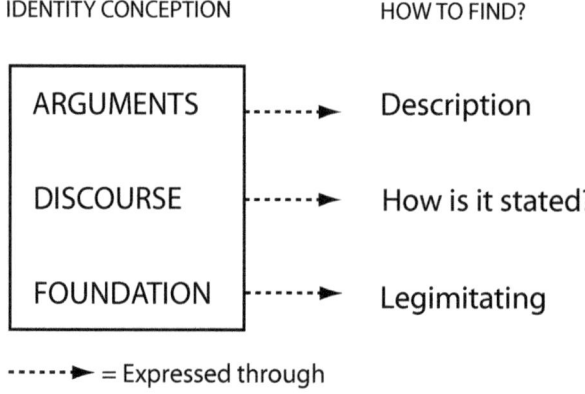

Figure 5.1 Scheme for analyzing conceptions of national identity

Arguments, discourse and foundation are defined in Chapter Two. We now turn to Mendès France's speeches during his time as Prime Minister (June 1954–February 1955). Through these speeches and other selected official material, aimed at different audiences, I seek to trace Mendès France's conception of France, the manner in which he defined the frontiers and borders of France and which power resources he identified as the legitimate foundations of the nation.[105] To that end, I shall apply three dichotomies (previously described in Chapter Three): the limits of national self-perception ("us – them"), the limits of national community ("member – outsider") and the limits of national values ("inclusive – exclusive"). These three dichotomies serve as tools to help reveal how Mendès France spoke about French identity. The dichotomies are not ideal

---

[105] I note key concepts at every level and at every dimension in every speech. I do not quantify in the text, but my analysis is based on both how often some key concepts are repeated and how central they are for the speech as such.

types, but instead reference points focusing the analysis on the essential elements of an identity conception. The objective is to discuss how Mendès France constructed his particular identity conception, using these dichotomies, in order to show how Mendès France conceptualized and filled the now empty concepts of "Us", "Member" and "Inclusive values" by using the negations of them. I might discover the frontiers and borders of his conceptions of, for example, "Us," by searching for whom he refers to as "them". I shall employ these approaches at all three levels.

Self-perception: US (or THEM)
National community: MEMBER (or OUTSIDER)
National values: INCLUSIVE (or EXCLUSIVE)

Figure 5.2 Analytical dimensions of the operative concept national self-image

Self-perception is the dimension in which I search for Mendès France's arguments, discourse and foundation about *France*. The issue is how an "Us-France" is separated from a "Them-not-France". Is it through ethnicity, history, territory, geography or values? Or is it through something else? I will try to define which the limits of "us" are.

National community is the dimension in which I search for Mendès France's arguments, discourse and foundation about the *national community*. A community could be defined as a group that is imagined to be historically tied together, a territory that has political unity, or simply a unit with political autonomy. It is important to establish how membership in the community is defined, as well as how an outsider is defined. My aim is to discover which resources Mendès France found most important for the definition of France as a national community.

National values comprise the dimension in which I search for Mendès France's arguments, discourse and foundation about *national values*. If national values are understood as universal values, rather than restricted to one's own community, then the values are inclusive. If, on the other hand, the national values are perceived as unique and inherently linked to one's own culture or nation, the result is exclusive values.

I have analyzed 26 of Pierre Mendès France's official speeches and notes, beginning with the investiture speech at June 17[th,] 1954 and ending with Mendès France's unsuccessful attempt to gain acceptance for his Algerian policy in the National Assembly on February 3rd, 1955. Ten of the speeches were presented before Assembly; eight are radio broadcasts; one is before the General Assembly of the United Nations; one is a press conference; one is a Party speech at the Congress of the Radical Party; one is an anniversary telegram; one is a speech at an official visit to Tunisia, and three are more or less official notes or telegrams to French officials.[106]

5.2   Conceptions of French identity: Arguments

How, then, did Pierre Mendès France describe France? Each of the three dimensions of the description (self-perception, national community, and national values) is discussed and analyzed below.

Pierre Mendès France deliberately addressed the population of France in his speeches. He perceived France as its population, its government, its citizens, and therefore also as his audience. In a radio broadcast following the peace treaty in Indochina (July 24, 1954), Mendès France announced that:

> ... la première mission dont le Parlement, en votre nom, m'avait chargé est maintenant accomplie.[107]

Further along in the same speech, he referred to the radio as

> ... ce contact permanent, cette association avec vous ...[108]

which means that mass media add a special value to the politics of France. In a speech before the Assembly (November 12, 1954) he asserted that all French citizens must enjoy the same position in the French community,

> ... sans distinction d'origine ou de religion ...[109]

Mendès France tended to described France with words and concepts such as loyalty, responsibility for future generations, and a central position in

---

106   All speeches could be found in Mendes France 1986 ("Gouverner, c'est choisir"). The speeches are: before l'Assemblé Nationale 17/6, 24/6, 26/6, 22/7, 10/8, 27/8, 12/11, 10/12, 20/12 1954 and 3/2 1955; radio speeches 18/6, 26/6, 10/7, 24/7, 31/7, 14/8, 18/9, 13/11 1954; telegrams 18/6, 26/6, 16/7 1954 and 4/1 1955; Speeches held in Tunis 31/7, and in the UN General Assembly 22/11 1954; Congress speech 16/10 1954; Declaration for the press 30/8 1954.
107   ... the first mission that the parliament, in your name, has entrusted me is now accomplished.
108   ... this permanent contact, this association with you ...
109   ... without distinction of origin or religion ...

a large community, but also with more traditional nationalistic symbols such as the state, the Republic and patriotism.

When his descriptions refer to frontiers and distinctions, Mendès France frequently uses concepts such as autonomy, the Union Française and sovereignty. He also mentions that France consists of those who wish to live and work within that community. In a radio broadcast on September 18, 1954, Mendès France said that

> C'est vous-mêmes qui vous créez des chances de vie meilleure et plus libre ...[110]

And in another speech (December 10, 1954) before the Assembly, he said in regards to who was and was not French in North Africa, that

> ...pour tous les Français attachés à leur pays, à son influence, à sa grandeur...[111]

it is clear that North Africa and metropolitan France has indissoluble ties. Mendès France describe the national community primarily as a value based community where autonomy and individual freedom are essential aspects, but manifest loyalty and a sense of affinity with the ideals of the nation are as important as formal attachment.

The national values at the centre of Pierre Mendès France's descriptions of France are peace, autonomy, unity and development. These values were viewed as the foundations national community, whether in France or another country. As he was introducing his new government (June 24 1954), Mendès France explained that...

> ... nous devions rechercher les moyens d'accroître, conformément à notre tradition libérale, l'autonomie de la population dont nous avons nous-mêmes organisé et voulu l'évolution ...[112]

Mendès France stresses stability, economic growth and welfare in his descriptions of both French values and values that ought to be prioritized globally. In his last parliamentary debate as Prime Minister (February 3, 1955) he rejected a message that only aimed at establish order in Algeria. Instead, he said, France must

---

110 It is you, yourselves that create your chances for a better life and more freedom as individuals ...
111 ... for all Frenchmen attached to their country, to its influence, to its grandeur ...
112 ... consistent with our liberal tradition, we have to search for ways to improve autonomy for the population which we ourselves are part of and want to develop ...

... agir dans le domaine économique, et enfin, le jour où l'ordre sera rétabli, et où la situation économique sera en progrès, nous pourrons envisager d'améliorer le fonctionnement des institutions politiques et des institutions administratives.[113]

Mendès France consistently described French national values as a platform for democracy and development.

Pierre Mendès France's *self-perception* of France at the argument level – his description of France, national community and national values – are primarily value based. History, territory, class, ethnicity or geography does not figure prominently in his discussions about French self perception. Instead, value based conceptions such as citizenship, autonomy, development or unity appear frequently. At the argument level, Mendès France's conception of "us and them" was value based. When it comes to *national community*, Mendès France's conception of membership in the community comprised all who shared his values and were prepared to work for them. His conception of an outsider was one who deliberately chose to stand aside. This conception distinguished Mendès France not only from many of his adversaries, whose conceptions of France usually were based on territory or history, but also from many of his colleagues, who (as discussed in Chapter Four) often held a conception that emphasized ethnicity or history. In the context of *national values,* Mendès France consistently described French national values as a platform for democracy and development. For him, autonomy and stability were essential for a nation to evolve both in terms of prosperity and influence. His values can be described as inclusive, since he intended them to apply universally.

5.3 Conceptions of French identity: Discourse

How is Mendès France's conception of France designed? Like the descriptions, the discourse regarding self-perception, national community and national values can be found in his speeches. But, searching for the discourse demands a sharp ear for both rhetoric and references that would have resonated easily with the audience during the period in question.

In his speeches, either on the radio or before the Assembly, Mendès France sought to engage the listeners in his own conception of France. He strove to make of himself and his listeners a collective, single actor, into a "we" rather than an "I" and a "you". There was very little polemic or

---

113 act in the economic domain, and when order is established, or when the economic situation is developing, we can expect to improve the functions of political and administrative institutions.

defensiveness in Mendès France's speaking style. He often appealed to a historical mission that he – and France – were mandated to fulfil, and he frequently referred to the future. It is clear that Mendès France aimed for national unity, but on the grounds of Republican and progressive values. He was focused on involving the listeners, whether they were ordinary citizens or parliamentary deputies. He argued that French political institutions – such as the National Assembly – were in themselves expressions of the national will. He therefore often placed the Assembly at the centre of his speeches, and insisted that it was the listeners who had the power to keep the Assembly at the heart of French politics. There is an implicit polemic against those who believe in strongmen and authoritarian leadership.

In Mendès France's interpretation, France is created in the moment when a bond of trust is established between the leader and the people. In his investiture speech, in regards to the peace in Indochina, (June 17, 1954) Mendès France insisted that

> Je sollicite votre confiance, dans ce seul but, pour une mission sacrée qui nous est dictée par le voeu ardent de la nation tout entière.[114]

He also noted the distinction between France on one side, and the Anglo-Saxons on the other. As the things in Viêt-nam has turned out Mendès France says, June 26, 1954, in a telegram to the French embassy in London and Washington that he hopes that the government of United States will hesitate with an aggressive reaction on a secession of Viêt-nam.

> Dans l'état actuel des choses, celle-ci ne peut conduire à aucun autre résultat qu'à ruiner tout espoirs de voir le Viêt-nam se consolider de façon à créer en face du Viêt-minh une force authentiquement nationale et indépendante[115]

But because of France's involvement in the war, Mendès France also made conventional remarks about French combattants, describing France's wounded soldiers as part of the body of the French nation. In a speech delivered on the radio on July, 3 1954, Mendès France spoke of "les premiers grands blessés" ("the first great casualties"), and in a speech before the National Assembly on July 22, he honoured "nos combattants" ("our

114 I need your confidence for that goal only, for this sacred mission which has been determined for us to fulfil by an ardent will of the whole nation.
115 In the current state of things, this (reaction, my remark) can lead to no other result that to ruin any hope to see Vietnam strengthening to create in front of Viêt-minh a force genuinely national and independent.

combatants") in Indochina with a moment of silence. Mendès France constructed a France that in its colonial ambitions also had to remain faithful to its heritage of promoting development and justice.

In his speech about the relationship between Tunisia and France in Tunis on July 31, 1954, Mendès France asserted that ...

> ... les reformes politiques seraient de peu portée si elles ne s'accompagnaient d'une action administrative, économique et sociale destine à améliorer les conditions d'existence du pays ...[116]

Representative democracy played an important role in Mendès France's rhetoric. He was always quick to point out that France's political institutions were expressions of France and of the French people's commitment to progress and change. In his speech at the Radical Party Congress on October 16, 1954, he clearly placed the Assembly at the centre of political life, stating that...

> ... le Parlement, interprétant la volonté nationale, à donné sa confiance à un gouvernement dont le but proclamé ... le redressement attendu par le pays.[117]

Because of his view of democracy, Mendès France's speeches frequently reflect a perspective where the individual is seen first and foremost as a citizen. Through a citizen-perspective, Mendès France discusses both colonial issues and economic policy. In a speech before the National Assembly, on November 12, 1954, he addressed every French citizen in Algeria, Muslims as well as Europeans, and openly called Frenchmen of Algerian descent "compatriots". In his speeches, Pierre Mendès France relied on his personal ability to build trust, confidence and hope in the creation of 'France'. Physical frontiers and boundaries were thus not as important as they had been if France had been created primarily through geography or history.

Mendès France stressed that his version of France was defined by the democratic process. On several occasions, he described his relationship with the French voters as a contract, one that must be fulfilled by both parties. The contract did not apply only within European France; Mendès France always included the territories outside of Europe (DOM-TOM) as

---

116 Political reforms do not mean anything if they are not accompanied with administrative, economic and social actions aiming at improving the conditions of living in the country ...
117 The parliament, interpreting the national will has given its confidence to a government which has as its only goal ... the waited national improvement.

5. PIERRE MENDÈS FRANCE AND THE CONCEPTION ...

well. In his first regular prime ministry radio message on Jun 18, 1954 he explicitly claimed:

> C'est avec émotion que je m'adresse aujourd'hui à vous tous qui m'écoutez dans la métropole et outre-mer.[118]

Mendès France saw the National Assembly as the core of democracy, and the boundaries of the Assembly were therefore also the boundaries of France. In the speeches of Mendès France, the national territory was described as something to be used for forging a value-based community, rather than something with a life of its own. In the National Assembly on July 22, 1954, just after the Geneva Conference, Mendès France emphasized that ...

> ... notre adversaire d'hier (the Viêt Minh in the North, my comment), ouvert dans nos écoles à nos formes de pensée, n'y restait pas insensible. Il a affirmé hier à Genève qu'il souhaitait le maintien de ses contacts économiques et culturels avec la France ...[119]

Mendès France thus differed markedly from many of his predecessors, who seemed to place much greater emphasis on the significance of territory itself. Georges Bidault, for instance, who negotiated in Geneva before Mendès France's arrival, was strongly opposed to the secession of Viêtnam. Mendès France was a proponent of a non-violent resolution, and willingly revealed his position. A national community, he believed, could not be founded on violence and fear, and required equality and understanding rather than rigid, hierarchic structures of obedience. In reference to the relationship between France and Tunisia in the National Assembly December 10, 1954, Mendès France explicitly stated ...

> Je ne suis pas partisan de la politique de force ...[120]

Mendès France included as members of the national community his listeners, all people of goodwill, and French citizens. He defined 'France' as a broad community, one from which you could exclude yourself, but would

118 It is with emotions I today address myself to everyone who listen in the heartland (metropole) and in the French territories and domains on the other side of the sea ...
119 Our adversaries of yesterday, opened in our schools to our forms of thought, did not remain insensible there. They have affirmed yesterday in Geneva that they wish to maintain the economic and cultural contacts with France ...
120 I am not a friend of the politics of force ...

not be excluded by him. When he stated that violence, mistrust and secession were not in line with his vision, he articulated an exclusion that was at the same time an inclusion: all those who did not believe in negative strategies such as violence were included in his vision. The manner in which he addressed people thus made them followers, although they did not buy all his political ideals or solutions.

Given his emphasis on solidarity, order and development as core national values, Mendès France could mistakenly be taken for a conventional nationalist. But his strong belief in technical development, progress, economic growth and planning indicates that his creation of a value-base for politics was far more complex. Mendès France often emphasised that construction, service, social and economic welfare were what politics were all about for a people that had suffered political betrayal. Introducing his new government on June 24, 1954, Mendès France announced that he had already convened a planning group at the Ministry of Finance. The Planning Group was tasked with formulating a schedule for the government's responsibilities prior to July 26. And on, July 31, discussing the Tunisian question before the Bey of Tunisia, Mendès France emphasised that ...

> Vous continuerez de trouver parmi eux tous les concours pour moderniser et développer votre royaume et pour vous aider à satisfaire les immenses besoins économiques et sociaux résultant de l'expansion démographique de votre people.[121]

He meant that without development, nothing else mattered much. Health, welfare, planning and economic growth are perhaps typically viewed as factors that erect borders between human beings, but Mendès France believed that these were the things that separated peoples from one another. He appealed to his listeners to recognise welfare as the first step towards unity and peace. Alongside his call for economic growth, Mendès France stressed that a global concern for peace and order was a necessary framework for development. In on of his last speech to National Assembly as Prime Minister, January 3–4, 1955 He said that

> ... l'ordre d'ailleurs, n'est pas pour nous une notion dissociable du progrès politique, économique et social. Mais il est vrai qu'aucune mesure d'ordre politique ou

---

[121] You will continue to find among them competitors for modernizing and developing your kingdom and helping you to meet and satisfy the immense economic and social needs that your rapid growth in population demands.

administrative qu'aucune précaution militaire et sera suffisante si nous n'apportant en même temps aux populations autochtones une aide rapide et massive contre le chômage et contre la faim.[122]

Through these conceptions, Mendès France thus rejected the notion of a narrow and solitary French national path, seeking instead to embrace other states as well as human beings in his mission.

Mendès France's discourse about *self-perception* was, then, all-encompassing. He allowed room for self-exclusion, yet did not exclude anyone himself. In regards to the *national community,* he addressed people as citizens, not as voters or individuals, and thereby offered them a bond of trust. He also interpreted France's political institutions as the expressions of the national political will. His mission was to bring stability and order to France, to facilitate progress, growth and welfare. He believed in an implicit contract that gave French citizens the right to dismiss him. In short, Mendès France cast himself as the servant of the people, a servant who needed the trust and loyalty of the public in order to accomplish his mission. In his discourse on *national values,* Mendès France strongly emphasised development, progress and planning, values that applied not only to European France, but to all peoples, including those in the former colonies.

5.4 Conceptions of French Identity: Foundations

What, then, were the legitimatising foundations for the mission that Mendès France created in his speeches? To construct the legitimate foundations of 'France,' Mendès France referred mainly to economic aspects, to a supranational will and various material resources. To construct a 'France' that has a self-perception that is accepted as legitimate he sometimes also goes back to patriotism.

Mendès France was clear on the importance of economic strength. In his investiture speech before the National Assembly on June 17, 1954 he made several references to the need for an active and progressive economic policy founded on financial rigor. Economic vitality would make it possible for France to assume the heavy burden of solidarity with peoples less fortunate than those of Europe. In his first radio speech as Prime Minister,

---

122 ... besides, order is for us certainly not dissoluble from political, economic and social progress. But, there are not any really sufficient political, administrative or military measures and precautions if they not meet the need for work and food for the population.

and in an implicit reference to de Gaulle's legendary June 1940 speech from London, Mendès France urged his listeners to

> ... lutter ensemble pour leur liberation ...[123]

But he also recognized that the development of France was inextricably tied to the Atlantic alliance. In a radio broadcast on July 10, 1954, in reference to the peace talks in Geneva, Mendès France noted that ...

> l'appui que nos amis et nos alliés nous apportent et qui a été confirmé dans le communiqué ...[124]

had been essential to progress in the negotiations. Movement required Western unity as well as abundant material resources. Mendès France was fully aware that the France of his visions necessitated a healthy economy. But colonial wars, domestic strikes and international disputes were disruptive to the economy and thus impeded any opportunity for genuine progress. A true strengthening of the French republic demanded first and foremost ...

> ... la volonté populaire active, vigilante, exigeante, stimulante à chaque instant pour les pouvoirs publics ...[125]

The element of self perception in the foundation thus had two dimensions, namely, the people's willingness to be engaged, and the material resources of the nation. This is what France had to legitimate her ambitions.

The legitimate grounds for membership in France were, according to Mendès France, created by a common culture and a willingness to unite The foundations of a national community were thus a readiness to cooperate and a desire to improve the state of the nation. In his radio speech of September 18, 1954, Mendès France argued that

> ... c'est vous mêmes qui vous créez des chances de vie meilleure et plus libre.[126]

---

123 ... fight together for our liberation ...
124 the support which our friends and allies has given us and which is confirmed in a communiqué ...
125 ... in every moment an active common will, vigilance, demands and bracing of public institutions ...
126 It is you yourselves that creates better chances for a better life and more freedom.

National presence was also an important fact, however. In some way, Mendès France understood the so-called "politics of presence" long before this concept was used in studies on representative government. Mendès France emphasized the importance of France's presence in both the Far East and North Africa. Yet he did not equate "presence" with "dominance". Speaking on the radio on July 31, 1954, about Tunisia, Mendès France announced that he wished to ...

> ... établir les bases d'une collaboration féconde dans l'estime et l'affection mutuelles.[127]

And speaking about Morocco before the National Assembly on August 27, 1954, he noted that ...

> La France se trouve en présence de deux État distincts de la République, quoique liés à elle, de populations dont nous n'avons jamais tenté de nier ou de réduire ni l'originalité nationale ni le génie propre.[128]

The foundations of legitimate separation – borders and boundaries – were therefore to be found in cultural and voluntary categories.

Mendès France appears to have placed peace above all other values. He viewed peace as a prerequisite for progress, speaking before the United Nations General Assembly on November, 22, Mendès France described the spirit of the United Nations as a norm for not only global, but also national action. He also referred to the Geneva Accords on Indochina, arguing that this treaty was proof that ...

> ... il est possible de négocier au lieu de se battre et que l'on peut se rencontrer avec le désir de s'entendre, au lieu de s'affronter pour se détruire.[129]

Alongside peace, however, he emphasised the importance of national sovereignty. In most of his speeches during this period, Mendès France stressed the values of national self-determination, autonomy, independence and sovereignty. In this aspect he could be viewed as more of a nationalist than a "globalist", but the value of independence was, during

---

127 ... establish bases for a fruitful collaboration in mutual esteem and affection.

128 France finds in both the states of the Republic, which ties them together, peoples that never tried to deny or reduce each other their uniqueness or their own wit.

129 ... it is possible to negotiate instead of fighting each other and that you can meet with the aim of understanding each other instead of confronting with destruction in mind.

this time, a double-edged sword. Mendès France was well aware of this when he employed the concept. For him, independence was a value for France, within Europe; but it was also a value for the territories in the Far East and North Africa. He believed in an 'inter-national' world where independent states cooperated with each other. He equated states with peoples, preferring not to address the dilemma of individuals who did not wish to belong to a certain people.

In many of his speeches, Mendès France's made clear that independence was not restricted to the old nation-states of Europe. Speaking about Tunisia in the National Assembly on August, 10 1954, Mendès France insisted that the French government had no intention of withholding from the Tunisians "l'exercice de souveraineté" ("the exercise of sovereignty"). And on July, 22 1954, in the immediate aftermath of the Geneva Accords on Indochina, Mendès France proclaimed that Laos and Cambodia had

> ... une constitution, un gouvernement, une indépendance indiscutable ...[130]

which already had been confirmed by the international community. Mendès France created a legitimate foundation for his conception of national identity by referring to values that lent themselves to unity – sovereignty, peace and progress. No one could credibly be opposed to these inclusive values, and Mendès France could thus use them to legitimate and gain wider acceptance for his mission.

In closing, the power sources that Mendès France considered most legitimate can be summed up as follows. In *self-perception,* Mendès France emphasised the economy, the national will and material resources as legitimating factors. These were the forces that could build up a legitimate 'France'. To define the legitimate borders of the *national community,* Mendès France used cultural and/or voluntary categories. A willingness to cooperate and improve the nation, a common cultural base and the desire to unite people were at the core of his conception of national community. In his approach to *national values,* legitimate power, and the foundations of national identity Mendès France stressed peace, progress and sovereignty. Mendès France believed these values to be cornerstones of French national identity, and were to transcend party borders and any other group affiliation. These values were therefore inclusive.

---

130 ...a constitution, a government, a undisputable independence...

5.5 Conclusion: Pierre Mendès France and the conception of national identity

In sum, Pierre Mendès France held a self-perception of France as an entity that could embrace anyone who wished to join; a view of national community as a tool for solidarity and common work, where the founding national values were independence, peace, stability and development, all aimed at universal application. I have summarized the basis for the analysis in Table 4.1.

Table 4.1 lists the key concepts I have used in the first stage of interpretation. These key concepts have been extracted from the speeches on the grounds of prominence, frequency of use, and emphasis. To find the creative and constructing parts of Mendès France's speeches, I searched for common meaning, sense, and significance in the message. My contention is that the key concepts below capture the essence of Mendès France's message. Reviewing the speeches again, with these key concepts in mind, I have been able to interpret the identity conception as it has been discussed in this Chapter.

Table 5.1 Pierre Mendès France's identity conception: key-concepts as interpreted from 26 speeches and other official statements.

	Self-perception	National Community	National Values
Arguments	Population Government Listeners	Autonomy Those who wish to take part Union Française	Peace Independence Development Unity
Discourse	Effort to engage people Historical mission to fulfil Future demands	Parliament central Territories as tools Non-violence	Technical development Progress Order and development
Foundation	Economy, National will Material resources	National effort Cooperation and improvement Unity in culture	Peace Economic and social progress Keep promises and contracts

My results and concluding interpretations are summarized below, in a simple table and brief description.

Table 4.2 The identity conceptions of Pierre Mendès France

ARGUMENT

Self-perception: US = the French population and its political institutions

National community: MEMBER = embraces all who wish to be inside the autonomic community

National values: INCLUSIVE = independence and development

DISCOURSE

Self-perception: US = anyone who is focused on the requirements of the future and a common mission

National community: MEMBER = not a question of territory but of solidarity with "US" as mentioned above

National values: INCLUSIVE = a belief in progress, rationality and modernity

FOUNDATIONS

Self-perception: US = where economic and material resources are available and increasing

National community: MEMBER = cultural unity is created when shared efforts and cooperation, not heritage or descent, are determinant

National values: INCLUSIVE = progress through fair legal processes and justice for all

---

To sum up my reasoning, the argument-level in Pierre Mendès France's identity conception is made up of a self-perception where the population and the political institutions occupy a central position; national community is depicted as autonomic and embracing; and the principal national values are independence and development through peaceful means. The discursive level is focused on a self-perception that emphasises meeting the demands of the future and the fulfilment of a mission; on a national community where territory is a tool rather than a criterion for solidarity; and on values where progress and development are the core. The foundational level, where Mendès France anchors his arguments, is made up of a self-perception where material and economic resources help legitimate the national identity, where cultural unity, cooperation and common efforts define the national community and the core values are peace, progress and a belief in justice and the rule of law.

Now is the time to explore and analyse how these identity conceptions, on several levels and held by several people and groups – analysed and established in Chapters Three, Four and Five – met and how these meetings figured in one Mendès France success (Indochina), and one Mendès France-failure (Algeria). In the next two Chapters, we will trace the Indochina context from the fall of Dien Bien Phu on May 7, 1954, to the peace treaty on July 20th of that same year. The subsequent chapter will focus on France's political treatment of Algeria from the eruption of unrest on November 1, 1954 until Mendès France's resignation on February 5, 1955.

6.
National Identity and French Indochina-policy 1954

We now turn to two prominent decolonisation cases in French history, namely Indochina and Algeria. The objective is to understand why Mendès France's policy in the case of Indochina was accepted, and indeed greeted with applause, while his approach to the Algeria question just months later was rejected and ridiculed.

We now know that Mendès France was quite alone in his conceptions of France. He rejected the idea that France should be defined primarily in terms of whether or not she was an empire, and focused instead on citizenship and belonging. The foundations for Mendès France's conception of French identity were economic resources, a unified cultural community, and belief in social progress and justice. The discourse of his identity conception was inclusive: All who wished to join the common societal efforts necessary to bring about modernity were welcome. Mendès France's argument stressed the bond between people and institutions. In his arguments, he also focused on national independence and development. This conception of France was – as shown in Chapter Four – incompatible with that of many of Mendès France's adversaries, particularly in regards to colonial issues, and was resisted even among his friends and collaborators. Nevertheless, Mendès France was able to solve the crisis in Indochina through a combination of forced, intensive negotiations and popular support. When he tried to apply the same identity conception to his policies on first Tunisia, and then Algeria, however, he failed. Why? His adversaries were the same, his conceptions remained unchanged. The conflict between his identity conception and that of others should therefore not have either increased or diminished.

In this Chapter, I discuss Pierre Mendès France and the Indochina War as follows. First, I focus on the war itself; then, I will describe the evolution of the political process surrounding Indochina. The analysis draws on primary sources from diplomatic archives. I will then identify turning points and decisive conflicts in the final phases of the decolonisation of Indochina. When and why did Mendès France initiate negotiations, thereby discarding many established truths and traditions? The chapter will conclude with my analysis of why Mendès France was successful in Indochina, despite many adversaries and a conception of France that conflicted with that of the French political elite.

6.1 From French Indochina to the American war in Vietnam[131]

Indochina fell under Japanese occupation during the Second World War. Although many had assumed that France would grant Indochina independence after the war, the French fought to re-establish their control in the area, engaging in warfare until 1954.

In 1887 France created the Indochina Union, comprising what are now Vietnam, Laos and Cambodia. Already before the Second World War, the Popular Front government in France, in which Pierre Mendès France participated, attempted to bring about reforms in Indochina. During the war, in 1941, Ho Chi Minh founded the Viet Minh, the political movement for Vietnamese independence. In 1944, General Vo Nguyen Giap created a military arm to the Viet Minh.

In September 1941 Japan occupied Indochina, but allowed the French Vichy government to administer the region. In March 1945, Japan assumed the administration of the area at the same time as the Vietnamese emperor Bao Dai proclaimed independence from France.

After the war was over in Europe, the Allied leaders (Churchill, Stalin, Truman and also Atlee) pressed Japan through a process of disarmament. Great Britain was engaged in South Vietnam, China in North Vietnam. But in the turbulent summer following the Potsdam Conference, Japan transferred power to the Viet Minh, Bao Dai abdicated and Ho Chi Minh proclaimed the independence of Vietnam. On September, 13, 1945, British forces landed in Saigon and returned political authority to France. France re-occupied Vietnam, but in the North (Tonkin) Ho Chi Minh's republican government demanded the unification of Vietnam, under Ho's leadership.

---

131 For an overview of the time see Chamberlain 1998, Berthier 1988 and www.skalman.nu/vietnam.

Through the Sainteny-Hô Chi Minh Accords, France recognized Vietnam as an autonomous state within the French Union, and promised a referendum on the question of the reunification of Vietnam. Three months later, without neither referendum nor negotiations, the French governor in Indochina proclaimed Cochinchina (southernmost Vietnam) independent. After negotiations between Ho Chi Minh and France, a sort of modus vivendi was reached. After a Vietnamese riot in Haiphong, however, avenged by the French in December 1946, a full-scale war erupted between the independence movement in Vietnam and France.

In 1949, the former Emperor Bao Dai persuaded France to support the idea of a unified Vietnam as an 'Associated State' within the French Union, and returned to Vietnam. Mao proclaimed the People's Republic of China that same year, however, and recognized the Democratic Republic of North Vietnam under the leadership of Ho Chi Minh in 1950. The United States and Great Britain recognized Bao Dai's government. China began to supply arms to Viet Minh army in the north. The Viet Minh met with a series of military successes, forcing the departure of France from the northernmost region (North Tonkin) after a disastrous defeat at Cao Bang. In June 1950 the Korean War erupted, and one month later, President Truman committed $15 million in military aid to help sustain France's war effort in Indochina.

In the summer of 1953 the Korean War ended with an armistice. In October of that year, France granted Laos full autonomy within the French Union. Prince Norodom Sihanouk declared Cambodia independent of France on November 9. The following month, Viet Minh forces entered Laos. In January 1954 the former Allies (including France) agreed to hold a conference on both Korea and Indochina, in Geneva.

On March 13, the fateful battle of Dien Bien Phu began. Dien Bien Phu was a French fort in northern Vietnam, near the border to Laos. The French hoped that they could sever the Viet Minh's supply and communication lines, but instead found themselves utterly surrounded and besieged. On May 7, Dien Bien Phu fell. Many experts mark this event as the turning point in France's vision of a French Indochina.

Negotiations opened in Geneva in April 1954, but were essentially deadlocked until Pierre Mendès France became Prime Minister. In July 1954, hostilities ceased, and Vietnam was divided at the 17th parallel. Free elections were to be held in Vietnam in two years. Only the military commanders actually signed anything, however, and the United States expressed dissatisfaction with various aspects of the agreement.

In October 1955 the Prime Minister in South Vietnam, Ngo Dinh Diem, defeated Bao Dai as president and proclaimed the new Republic of

Vietnam. It was now that the long struggle between the two Republics of North and South Vietnam began. The French withdrew from Vietnam over the course of 1955 and 1956, while Diem began the persecution of Viet Minh sympathisers in the South. In 1960 North Vietnamese leaders formed the Viet Cong (FNL) to free South Vietnam and unify the country. US advisers remained in South Vietnam after the departure of the French. The Hanoi regime enjoyed the support first of Russia, and of China as of 1963. The conflict in Vietnam soon escalated to a confrontation between the superpowers, the United States supporting the South, and Russia backing the North. In 1962 the US presence increased significantly. The following year, South Vietnam was shaken by the assassination of Diem and his brother, followed by the establishment of a military government under General Duong Van Minh.

On August 2, 1964 North Vietnam attacked an American warship, the USS Maddox, in international waters in the Gulf of Tonkin. Within a few days, the US Congress approved (with only two votes opposed) a resolution granting the President the power to prevent by any means necessary, and without further Congressional approval, any aggression against American troops or South Vietnam. Through the Tonkin Gulf Resolution, the United States was de facto at war in Vietnam.[132] The war did not end until 1975, when the Americans withdrew and Vietnam was unified under a single Communist regime.

6.2 The year of 1954 – Defeat and surrender

Pierre Mendès France had been a prominent critic of Conservative policies in Indochina since the early days of the conflict. He rose to power largely on the promise to end this increasingly unpopular war. To understand the process, we must go back to 1953. In November of that year, the garrison at Dien Bien Phu had been recaptured from the Viet Minh by French air troops.[133] There were twelve battalions at Dien Bien Phu, and the fort served used primarily as an air-base and a northern stronghold to control Viet Minh transports and support in Laos and the Tonkin area. General Navarre, the French military commander in Indochina, had discussed the fort publicly, and it was believed that the Viet Minh's General Giap could not manoeuvre a sufficient number of troops through the northern jungles to seriously threaten Dien Bien Phu.

---

132 Compare Neu 2003.
133 Background from Clayton 1994.

The Viet Minh constructed roads and communications around Dien Bien Phu, however, and in the end had amassed some 60 000 soldiers around the fort. On March 13, the Viet Minh launched an attack on Dien Bien Phu, and within days the French airstrips were under fire, interrupting the airborne supplies on which the French troops depended. The French soldiers were left with no means to defend themselves; they struggled in vain. On the evening of May 7, 1954, Dien Bien Phu fell. But throughout the battle of Dien Bien Phu, the Geneva Conference proceeded as scheduled.

The Geneva Conference had been initiated at the most recent Berlin Conference, an annual event that brought together France, the UK, the US, and the Soviet Union. The Geneva Conference was to focus on international questions such as Korea and Indochina. Before the Conference opened, France requested military assistance from the US for the war in Indochina, but after a number of diplomatic discussions, President Eisenhower denied the request. Eisenhower and Churchill agreed that no action should be taken on the matter at this time. After the surrender of Dien Bien Phu, many French officers believed they had been betrayed by the US, a feeling that intensified when US troops took over the conflict in Indochina a few years later.[134]

The Geneva Conference opened on April, 26, 1954. The French delegation, headed by Georges Bidault, refused to consider the partition of Vietnam or any form of negotiation with the Viet Minh. Even the fall of Dien Bien Phu did not alter Bidault's views on these issues. While it was clear that a military withdrawal was inevitable, France insisted that only the United States could replace France in Vietnam.

In a note from General Navarre about the military situation before the Geneva Conference, the French strategy in Dien Bien Phu was described as an effort to "réduire la grande tâche viet minh isolée du reste du territoire ennemi."[135] ("reduce the large Viet Minh contingent that was isolated from the rest of the enemy territory.") But in the same document, it is stated that the French strategy is mainly a defensive one, an attempt to prevent the escalation of hostilities. Already in 1950, the French military insisted that its position in Indochina was disastrous, and that France had suffered a "véritable hémorragi" ("a true haemorrhaging") in Indochina since 1945.[136] Time and again, military commanders urged their govern-

---

134 Clayton 1994 p. 75.

135 Note sur la situation militaire en Indochine à la veille de la conférence de Geneve" April 21, 1954. Dossier "Indochina".

136 Note from General Blanc to Ministre Dec 19, 1950. Dossier "Indochine".

ment to request the assistance of the United States in Indochina and to begin conscription in France to supplement the shrinking troops. The Commander in Saigon, General Blanc, wrote as late as February 8, 1954 that withdrawing from Indochina was not an option, since this would amount to abandoning the territory to the Communists and betraying the ideals of l'Union Française.[137]

On March 22, the situation at Dien Bien Phu had become quite serious, and in a telegram to Paris the military at Dien Bien Phu urged for airborne attacks with "l'emploi massif du napalm" ("the massive use of napalm."). The enemy was described as having overpowered the French troops and taken the terrain by heavy artillery.[138] The same day, General Navarre wrote to Foreign Minister Georges Bidault and claimed that the war was now lost, but that the Geneva Conference "vaut cette réintensification de la guerre"("is worth the re-intensification of the war").[139] In the diplomatic archives, there are a number of documents that discuss the introduction of conscription in France if the Geneva Conference did not yield any acceptable resolution.

Just before the French government resigned in June 1954, the military situation was such that the only assistance French soldiers could receive was from so-called voluntary soldiers from the US, who could be hired by French units. No official help was extended by the United States, despite overt demands for assistance. On the eve of the Geneva Conference, there were some indications that the Soviet Union was ready to shift its position. Moscow seemed prepared to consider a divided Indochina, an option it had categorically rejected earlier. As the French saw it, the positions of the key powers were as follows. Great Britain and France were prepared to negotiate, the US did not seem to think it was worth the time, and the Soviet Union was reluctant to accept any solution that did not involve a full French surrender. The US also was not prepared to risk its relations with China, which had supplied the Viet Minh with arms since 1950.[140]

After Dien Bien Phu, the French goals at the Geneva Conference were peace in Laos and Cambodia, and international control over Vietnam with guarantees of political unity and future free elections. To obtain a ceasefire, France agreed to regroup its troops in Indochina, without actually having to withdraw. French negotiator Bidault asked Secretary of State

137 General Lattre, Note January 1951. Comité de Chef d'Etat-Major August, 25 1951, Note. General Blanc, Note, February, 8 1954. All in dossier "Indochine".
138 Saigon to French foreign ministry, Paris March 22, 1954 at 21.50. Dossier "Indochine".
139 Letter from Navarre to Minister March, 23 1954. Dossier "Indochine".
140 Note, Ministre des Affaires Etrangères, A.S. Conference de Genève, June 29, 1954. Dossier "Indochine".

John Foster Dulles what the US might do if, contrary to French hopes, the Geneva Conference failed to bring about an end to the war. In response, the US introduced seven conditions that would have to be met before the US would consider intervening directly:

1. Demand for assistance from the French government together with Laos, Cambodia and Vietnam.
2. The same demand from these countries to Thailand, the Philippines, Australia, New Zealand and the UK.
3. UN support for the contribution.
4. Independence for the three countries in Indochina, guaranteed by the US.
5. Maintenance of French military presence at the same level as when the intervention begins.
6. Arrangement for the organisation of the intervention
7. A ratification of the intervention from the French National Assembly.[141]

A number of these conditions were virtually impossible to meet. The French delegation tried to negotiate with the US on several of these points, and it was in this context that the partition of Vietnam was first seriously discussed. In the end, however, the US made clear that an intervention could not occur before they had the chance of making their own considerations for an intervention on the ground in Indochina.[142] On June, 18 1954, the talks came to an end and the Foreign Ministers and representatives returned home. But thanks to the French delegation, the Conference was not formally dissolved.

The spring of 1954 had been a disaster for France and for the French Union. In Dien Bien Phu, France had suffered 16 000 casualties – 2 000 dead, 3 000 wounded, 11 000 missing in action. Between 1945 and 1954, a total of nearly 100 000 soldiers died on the Indochina front – 21 000 French, 12 000 legionnaires, 15 000 North Africans, 28 000 Indochinese and 18 000 from other parts of the French Union.[143] The French delegation, led by French negotiator Bidault, recognized that it could not secure US support for goals imposed by France, and that the military position in Indochina was lost. France had also remained unwilling to negoti-

---

141 Note, Ministre des Affaires Étrangères, A.S. Conference de Genève, June 29, 1954, p. 11. Dossier "Indochine".

142 Note, Ministre des Affaires Étrangères, A.S. Conference de Genève, June 29, 1954, p. 12. Dossier "Indochine".

143 Statistical reports, July 1954. Dossier "Indochine".

ate directly with the Viet Minh. Bidault's objective was an independent Vietnam, not the abandonment of the country to the Communists. The period leading up to June 18 had also been filled with discussions on the possibility of a US intervention – a rather unattractive prospect for a United States that was already entangled in the situation on the Korean peninsula, and was reluctant to damage its relationship with China.

The turning points during this period were the French collapse at Dien Bien Phu and Secretary Dulles' formulation of the seven conditions for a US intervention. The seven conditions made it clear to France that a US intervention, based on a French analysis of the situation, was not possible. But France had no other suggestions to make. For the French military, although defeated, and the French representatives at Geneva, the presence of France in Indochina was not negotiable. The Geneva process was for them a discussion on how to bring Indochina under the control of the western states, not on how to make peace in the area.

6.3 The year of 1954 – the success of Mendès France

Pierre Mendès France was inaugurated as Prime Minister of France on June 18, 1954, days after the government headed by Joseph Laniel resigned. Mendès France promised he would solve the Indochina crisis within one month. In the ensuing section of this Chapter, I will analyse the political and negotiation process and bring to light the conflicting interests and identities that were expressed during that month.

The key actors in this process were Pierre Mendès France, US Secretary of State John Foster Dulles, British Foreign Minister Anthony Eden, Soviet Foreign Minister Molotov, Viet Minh chief representative Pham Van Dong, Chinese Prime Minister Chou en-Lai, the French delegation headed by Jean Chauvel in Geneva, and, to some extent, the military commission headed by General Ely and Colonel Brébisson. Before Mendès France's government, there had been no question of opening a dialogue with the Viet Minh, although after Dien Bien Phu and Dulles' seven conditions, it seems that Georges Bidault began considering the idea, however vaguely.[144] The US was not keen on making a peace they did not think fair, and the Soviet Union was more focused on getting France ousted from Indochina than on the possible consequences of such an outcome. China had been reluctant, although it supported the Viet Minh with arms, because it feared that the total withdrawal of France might imply the arrival of a

144 Clayton 1994 p. 71 note 17.

US contingent in South Vietnam. The Viet Minh negotiator Pham Van Dong did not accept the partition of Vietnam as a solution. When Mendès France assumed the duties of Prime Minister, he committed himself to obtaining a satisfactory treaty in Geneva within one month, or he would agree to conscription for the Indochina War and resign.

On June 20, Mendès France met with US negotiator Walter Bedell-Smith and told him that France wished to resume negotiations. Though the US was suspicious, and anxious not to be trapped into a "bad peace," Mendès France insisted.[145] He convened with British Foreign Secretary Anthony Eden at the British Embassy in Paris, and then travelled to Geneva to meet with Bedell-Smith, Prime Minister Dinh-Diem of the government of Vietnam, and Nguyen De from the Bao Dai cabinet. A few days later, Mendès France continued on to Bern to visit with Chou en Lai at the French Embassy.

The French military commission in Geneva, now headed by General Ely, initially did not support the division of Vietnam. As the negotiations began, the French military argued that a divided Vietnam could be dangerous both for the French army and for the Vietnamese soldiers fighting on the French side.[146] But already the next day, Jean Chauvel, France's chief representative in Geneva, said in a private meeting with his team that "il ne semble pas y avoir d'autre solution que le partage du Vietnam" ("There appears to be no other solution than the partition of Vietnam.").[147] And in a telegram to the French Embassies in London and New York, Mendès France claimed that the objective of France was to accept a partition of Vietnam aimed at peace and the subsequent restructuring of the Vietnamese state. He asked the US not to encourage any anti-partition protests in the south of Vietnam, but instead to urge the Diem government in Saigon to accept this solution.[148] The French military commission in Geneva had no choice but to accept the partition – but only as far south as the 18th parallel, though the Viet Minh wanted to divide Vietnam at the 13th. The important point was that the partition of Vietnam was now on the agenda. Archival sources indicate that this solution was Mendès France's contribution. And that contribution marked a turning point in the Geneva Conference.

This interpretation is not unchallenged, however. In an exchange of

---

145 Transcript of recorded interview with PMF June 17 1964 for the John Foster Dulles oral history project, Princeton University, Dr P.A.Crowd. Dossier "Indochine" Vol V.
146 Note June 23, 1954, Dossier "Indochine" Vol V.
147 Note, June 24, 1954, Dossier "Indochine" Vol V.
148 Telegram, June 26, 1954, from PMF to London/New York. Dossier "Indochine" Vol V.

letters and a number of official speeches, one of Mendès France's most prominent adversaries, M. Frederic-Dupont, claimed that it was Colonel Brebisson (one of the leaders of the French military commission in Geneva) who on June, 17 1954 first suggested the partition of Vietnam. Frederic-Dupont argued that the Viet Minh representative was at that time prepared to accept the division of Vietnam at the 18th parallel, and that Mendès France squandered the opportunity. Brebisson claimed that the discussion on partition constituted a hypothetical situation and that the solution was not anchored in the Viet Minh leadership.[149]

Other sources claim it was Anthony Eden who forced Molotov to accept the idea, and that Molotov then persuaded Pham Van Dong, the Viet Minh negotiator, that a partition was a reasonable solution.[150]

In his biography of Pierre Mendès France, Jean Lacouture insists that Mendès France introduced the idea of partition at his June 23 meeting with Chou en Lai in Bern. The Chinese Prime Minister had stressed that the military situation was far more urgent than the political one, upon which Mendès France asked him if he would consider "la formule de regroupement militaire par 'très larges zones'" ("a military regrouping on the basis of very large zones."). The choice of words makes it implicit that these large zones amounted to a partition of the land.[151]

After the meeting with Chou en Lai, Mendès France was invited to talk with the Viet Minh representative Pham Van Dong. The head of the French negotiation team, Jean Chauvel, had already met unofficially with Van Dong, and discussed the possibility of a partition at the 13th parallel. General Ely was against any form of partition, but was he forced to accept one; the only defendable frontier would be the 18th parallel.[152]

Faced with this tenuous situation, Mendès France turned to Washington in an effort to bring high-level US representation back to Geneva. Dulles

---

149 Letters and notes from E. Frederic-Dupont and colonel Brebissison, Dossier "Indochine" Vol VI. *L'Année politique* 1954 p. 292.
150 Busch 2003 p. 4.
151 Lacouture 1981 p. 239.
152 Note, Commission Militaire, July, 10 1954. Dossier "Indochine" Vol V.

refused to return to the negotiations, stating that the Viet Minh had not yet demonstrated any "goodwill". Hours after Dulles' response, the Viet Minh delegation and the delegation of Vietnam (South) convened. Mendès France invited Dulles to Paris to meet with himself and Eden. Dulles arrived in the middle of the night on July 12, and engaged in lengthy talks with Mendès France and Eden. A decisive factor for Dulles was that Mendès France would not yield to the Viet Minh. The discussion on partition proceeded favourably.[153] The conclusion was that the United States agreed to re-engage in the Geneva Conference with high-level representation, through Walter Bedell-Smith. This marked the second turning point in the negotiations. Since Molotov earlier had agreed to return as well, all of the key parties were back in Geneva in the middle of July 1954. And the new issue at hand was how to partition Vietnam.

By the time that Dulles agreed to come to Paris, Pham Van Dong was already focused on negotiating the new frontier, and on July 13, the Viet Minh delegation had revised its request: it would accept partition at the 16th, rather than the 13th, parallel.[154]

It was clear that Vietnam was going to end up divided. The only question was at which latitude. In discussions with Molotov, Mendès France insisted on the 18th parallel. But in the final hours, Molotov made his own contribution. When Eden, Chou en Lai and Molotov met with Pham Van Dong to persuade him to set a date for elections in Vietnam, and perhaps agree to moving the frontier, Molotov proposed the 17th parallel as a compromise solution.[155] Pham Van Dong thought it best to accept. After a brief discussion on the timing of the elections (within two years), the agreement was reached.

The first turning point in the negotiations was the introduction of the idea of partition. Once this suggestion was on the agenda, negotiations could resume. The second turning point was the decision by Secretary of State Dulles to come to Paris and then agree to send a high-level delegation back to Geneva. The decision to negotiate directly with Pham Van Dong, and the successful talks with Chou en Lai, were important events as well. But it is unlikely that they would have been of much significance if the idea of partition had not been introduced, and if the United States had not returned to the negotiations.

---

153 Eisenhower 1963 p. 370.
154 Note, Dossier "Indochine" Vol V. Mendès France 1986 vol III p. 119. But Lacouture claims that it was Chou en Lai that did the concession, Lacourure 1981 p. 248.
155 Lacouture 1981 p. 255.

The French military was in no position to seriously oppose the partition, given their grave defeat at Dien Bien Phu. But this did not mean that General Ely (and his predecessor General Navarre) believed that France had definitively lost Indochina. There is ample evidence that the military sought a solution, backed by the United States, where France would remain in Indochina. The aim was to contain the Communists in the North and to contribute to a French strategic position in the world. Preserving the strength of the French Union was also an important value in and of itself. General Blanc, Commander of the Armed Forces in France, was sent by his government to Indochina in January 1954. Upon his return, Blanc concluded that France should establish a political order in Indochina before terminating the conflict. He also insisted that France should not turn Indochina over to the Communists, which would amount to abandoning a strategic centre of the French Union as well as betraying the people of Vietnam who trusted France to protect them.[156]

The French military had emphasised the importance of US assistance since already in 1951. In a note from the Comité de Chefs d'Etat-Major to the government on August, 25 1951, US support was described as "la seule solution" ("the only solution"), along with an upgrading of the Vietnamese army.[157] For the military, Indochina was a strategic territory within the French Union, and the people there required protection from Communist encroachment. But nowhere among the military elite was Indochina perceived as a part of France or as a historical territory with cultural and ethnic connections to metropolitan France.

Among the leadership, Indochina was seen primarily as a territory of strategic importance in the struggle against Communism in the whole of Southeast Asia.[158] For Mendès France, Indochina was a territory as such, and its citizens were either French citizens or Vietnamese individuals who had the right to determine their own destiny. In a telegram to General Ely dated July 16, 1954, Mendès France expounds on his thoughts on a divided Vietnam. His hope was that South Vietnam would be sufficiently strong to reunite the country in the elections of 1956. The involvement of France, however, was to be limited to the economic realm and to the protection of French soldiers.

The independence of Vietnam would be supported with technical support and economic aid. Nowhere in the telegram is there a glimpse of an

---

156 Letters from General Blanc February 8 and 28 1954. Dossier "Indochina" Vol IV.
157 Note, August, 25, 1951. Dossier "Indochina" Vol IV.
158 Eisenhower 1963 p. 333.

identity conception that includes Vietnam in the French national identity. The identity elements that Mendès France puts forth are those he always emphasised – economic resources, social progress and a conception of the national community based on political institutions and voluntary belonging.

Neither the Chinese, Soviet, US nor British conceptions of national identity were up for discussion. Mendès France had mainly to play a domestic game, forcing his conceptions on the French military in order to demonstrate, particularly to the United States, that France was prepared to find a solution to the war that would be acceptable to Washington. Instead of demanding US military help to fight the war, Mendès France requested US support for a solution that would grant Indochina its independence, and pave the way for a democratic, unified state. Mendès France was able to do this because the French military had lost the war long before Dien Bien Phu, and therefore was politically disarmed. He was also able to do this since his own conception of French national identity did not necessitate French control over the Indochinese territory.

The turning points in the process were, in essence, effects of Mendès France's identity conception – a conception he may have believed had gained wide acceptance by the time the Geneva Accords were signed on July 20, 1954.

6.4 The year of 1954 – the aftermath

It is often said that the United States did not sign the Geneva Accords of 1954.[159] But the truth is that none of the high-level representatives did.[160] The Geneva Accords consisted of three elements: three accords about cease-fire, an exchange of letters between Mendès France and Pham Van Dong, and a final declaration with thirteen points involving all of the participants. Instead of jeopardizing the fragile consensus by trying to persuade the US and China to sign the same paper, the signatories (Laos, Cambodia and France) made statements with reference to the final declaration. In addition, there were several declarations made with reference to the final declaration that was not comprised in the Accords.

In its declaration, the United States made clear that it agreed with the principles of the United Nations and would do nothing to disturb or obstruct the implementation of Accords. Bedell-Smith added that the US

---

159 The agreement is dated July, 20 1954 at 2400 but was signed July, 21.
160 Lacouture 1981 p. 261.

would react to any aggression against the Accords "with grave concern," viewing it as a threat to international peace and security.[161] The final declaration stipulated that free elections would be held in Vietnam in July 1956, a statement that the South Vietnamese government rejected with reference to its right to determine its own future as a unified state. The United States was of the same opinion. It is also obvious that the representative from the South Vietnamese government, Tram Van Do, in no way agreed with the conditions for peace and the partition of Vietnam. He underlined that the French government has assumed the right to command Vietnamese soldiers and to "abandon" the territories in the north to the Viet Minh.[162]

The day of the Geneva declarations, US President Eisenhower gave a press conference where he stated that the US was not "bound by the decisions taken at the Conference" and that the US would actively "pursue discussions with other free nations to establish an organization of collective defence" in Southeast Asia.[163]

The outcome of the Geneva Accords was not what might have been hoped for. In the middle of the summer of 1954, Jean Sainteny was installed as the representative to the French government in North Vietnam. His mission was to facilitate trade and cultural exchange between France and the Democratic Republic of Vietnam. Mendès France underlined that the French presence was "sur un plan consulaire de présence, de maintien de nos intérêts culturels, de protection de nos ressortissants et de leur bien. Elle n'a donc pas un caractère politique. ("... on a consular level only, to maintain our cultural interests, to protect the members of our state and their well-being. It is not of a political nature.")"[164] France sought to establish amicable relations with North Vietnam, and North Vietnam had reason to reciprocate: In October, Sainteny advised Paris of a recent meeting with Ho Chi Minh, where Ho Chi Minh had stated that he desired a "certaine indépendance" ("a certain independence") from other Communist states, and hoped that France would help.[165] In Paris there were some concerns that Sainteny was more of a channel from Hanoi to Paris, than a channel from Paris to Hanoi.[166]

While relations between North Vietnam and France improved, relations

161 L'Année politique 1954 p. 592. The formulation "threat to international peace and security" means that the UN have mandate to intervene. Compare Bring 1974 p. 77ff.
162 L'Année politique 1954 p. 593.
163 Esienhower 1963 p. 371. The pact in Southeast Asia later became SEATO.
164 Instructions from Mendès France, August, 23, 1954. Dossier "Indochine" Vol V (2).
165 Report from Sainteny to Guy de La Chambre, Octobre, 21 1954. Dossier "Indochine" Vol VII.
166 Note, Cheysson to Mendès France, November, 2 1954. Dossier "Indochine" Vol V (2).

between South Vietnam and France deteriorated. Relations between the United States and France were troubled as well. Mendès France claimed that the South Vietnamese government, under Ngo Dinh Diem, ignored the need for reforms. Dulles in turn argued that South Vietnam needed a solid nationalist government and that the US was committed to supporting Diem to prevent Communist infiltration. It was essential, in Dulles' view that South Vietnam understands that the free world was behind his government.[167] The US was also sceptical of the idea of giving Laos, Cambodia and Vietnam a national responsibility for requesting military support if they needed it. France responded by insisting that the Geneva Accords be respected, which meant that there could be no US command of Vietnamese forces. Meanwhile, the French military in Saigon was also suspicious of France's friendly relations with Hanoi. General Ely did not think that France gives the Saigon-government the best thinkable chance in the coming elections 1956.[168]

Mendès France found himself confronted with a dilemma. If he supported the position of the French military and of the United States, and allowed a US command in South Vietnam, he would arouse suspicion in Hanoi and therefore forfeit his position as broker; if he supported Hanoi, both French public opinion and Washington would question his motives, and he would forfeit his position as trusted policy maker. Mendès France was loyal and faithful to the Accords in that he wished for both parts of the divided country to have the same opportunities in the elections. He had no ulterior motives for the elections, and was even prepared for a possible Viet Minh victory. But he claimed that Diem's government was not the least interested in France's policy in Indochina.[169] In February 1955, France and the US determined their relations to the Vietnamese army in accordance with the Geneva documents, which meant that there would be no US military command.

The aftermath of the Geneva Accords could well be summarized with the words of Claude Cheysson and Jean Chauvel in their report on Indochina to the new Prime Minister, Edgar Faure, in February 1955:

> La politique menée au nord-Vietnam a été régulièrement portée à la connaissance des Américains. Ceux-ci sans marquer un grand enthousiasme ne se sont élevés

167 Letter from J F Dulles to p. Mendès France, August, 19 1954. Translated to French. Dossier "Indochine" Vol VI.
168 Note from General Ely to Pierre Mendès France, December 31, 1954. Dossier "Indochine" Vol VII.
169 Note p. Mendès France to Guy de la Chambre, January, 4, 1955. Dossier "Indochine" Vol V (2).

contre aucune des mesures prises par la France. (...) ... la France ne devait pas risquer une dispute grave avec le gouvernement américain en menant au sud-Vietnam une politique indépendante de celle des États-Unis.[170]

The conflicts that were obviously simmering beneath the surface would soon prove serious and dangerous to the future of Vietnam. General Diem failed to implement reforms in South Vietnam, provoking France. The French claimed that Diem was ruining the possibility of uniting Vietnam through free elections and attempting to force his policies on North Vietnam. France feared that Diem's approach would result in the permanent partition of Vietnam, with North Vietnam drawing ever closer to the Communist bloc. To avoid such a development, Paris made every effort to maintain friendly relations with Hanoi. Washington in its turn found France to be wavering in its support of the free world and the struggle against Communism. The US wished to support the nationalist regime in Saigon, even if this required a US military command, and was far less interested in the circumstances surrounding the coming elections in Vietnam or in the Geneva Accords.

As we now know, there were no elections in Vietnam in 1956, and the war flared up again beginning in the 1960s. It was not until 1975 that the Vietnamese people were able to live in peace.

6.5 Conclusion

Besides the war itself, the main conflict in the decolonisation of Indochina was between two points of view. One was Mendès France's conception of Vietnam as a future independent nation-state with close ties to France, where no effort should be spared to mobilize the people on behalf of the Geneva Accords, and with an eye towards peace, progress and development. The other was the US conception (shared by the French military in Saigon) of a strategic territory in the struggle of the free world against Communism, where no effort should be spared to support the ideologically kindred government in Saigon so that Vietnam could one day be unified on its terms.

In France, public opinion had clamoured for an end to the war. Even Mendès France's domestic adversaries conceded that he had acted well in

---

170 "The policy implemented in North Vietnam has regularly been made known to the Americans. Though they have not shown great enthusiasm, they have not opposed any of the measures taken by France. (...) ... France should not risk a serious dispute with the American government by conducting a policy in South Vietnam that is independent of the policy of the United States."

bringing the conflict to an end. There were no strong opinions in regards to either Vietnam's future or how to preserve the influence of France in Indochina. This was why Mendès France's conception of national identity met with little resistance. The only true opposition came from the United States, and when Mendès France resigned as Prime Minister in February 1955, the US was liberated from its obligations to him. And in France the war in Algeria was emerging as the next great dilemma.

My conclusion is that Mendès France negotiated and implemented the Geneva Accords on the grounds of his own conception of national identity. His conception was founded on the notions of national will, cultural unity and social progress. He believed in an actively involved citizenry and in political institutions as the guarantors of justice. He advocated national autonomy and addressed himself to all who wished to join the community. This conception, discussed in detail in Chapter Five, did not jeopardize his position despite that the other participants at Geneva did not share his view. The French military, which certainly did not share his conceptions, had been defeated and had lost its political influence. French opinion wanted an end to the war for both economic and human reasons, and feared the introduction of conscription. The US, which also did not share his view, was focused on fighting the Communists in Indochina and believed this could better be done through a peace that gave Saigon ample economic and military aid. The Hanoi government could secure a large span of contiguous territory, a far more favourable solution than earlier suggestions of dividing the country into enclaves. China needed recognition from the UN and had been damaged by the Korean War, and also feared that if the French withdrew completely, they would be replaced by a US presence.

The outcome of the Indochina War shows, in my view, that Mendès France's conception formed the basis of the Geneva Accords in 1954. He may not, however, have realised that the other parties had other motives for their attachment to the Geneva Accords. His conception was not met with serious opposition, and therefore was not tried by perseverant adversaries. In reality, the end of the Indochina War was informed by very different motivations – something that became evident only a few months after the Accords had been reached.

7.
National Identity and French North Africa Policy 1954–1956

Mendès France was not as successful in North Africa as he had been in Indochina. It was his attempt to formulate a new foreign policy towards North Africa that ultimately brought him down.

The Maghreb region was structured into two different kinds of relations with France. Algeria was considered a part of metropolitan France and as such was governed by France's Ministry of the Interior. Tunisia and Morocco were protectorates under the jurisdiction of the Foreign Ministry. None of the territories were thus "colonies" in the strict sense, as Indochina had been. The focus of this chapter is French policy towards North Africa and towards Algeria in particular, since this was the most prominent political issue in France in the late 1950s. Tunisia and Morocco gained independence in 1956, but Algeria was subjected to a cruel war before independence was granted in July 1962. French policy towards Tunisia and Morocco was nonetheless important because it communicated a certain model for independence – and that model was drafted first by Mendès France.

We now know that Mendès France used his conception of France in his negotiations on Indochina, and that this conception did not cause any upheaval despite the different motives of the negotiation parties. But in North Africa the situation was somewhat different. Mendès France's conception of France, which emphasised belonging and citizenship, included Algeria and its population of diverse descent. Mendès France's focus on national independence and sovereignty implied that Morocco and Tunisia had the right to govern themselves. As shown earlier, Mendès France's conception of France was incompatible not only with that of his adversaries, but also with the conceptions of many of his allies. Despite this,

Mendès France was able to negotiate a resolution to the Indochina war. But in regards to North Africa, it seemed that any move towards granting independence to Tunisia and Morocco was beyond what could be accepted. Mendès France's identity conceptions were the same as they had been during the Indochina negotiations, which in fact were taking place around the same time as policy towards North Africa was being developed. But in discussions on North Africa, Mendès France's conceptions of national identity became too explicit somehow, and were perceived as too great of a challenge to the conceptions held by others in France's foreign-policy elite.

In this chapter, I analyse the policy of France and of Pierre Mendès France towards North Africa, from the speech at Carthage in July 1954 to Mendès France's final resignation in May, 1956. I begin with a brief overview of relations between North Africa and France. Thereafter, I describe the evolution of Mendès France's policy. For this discussion, I rely on primary sources obtained from historical archives. First, I will discuss the year 1954 – with a brief glance ahead to February 1955. The subsequent section focuses on the spring of 1956, when Mendès France was again a government actor dealing with policy towards Algeria. The focus here is on turning points and decisive conflicts in the development of the policy. I conclude with a discussion about why Mendès France's approach to North Africa failed, while his policy on Indochina succeeded.

7.1 From a "war against pirates" to an independent Maghreb

In the early years of the 19th century, pirates tormented the Mediterranean region. The French king Charles X was able to exploit this, diverting public opinion from domestic problems by highlighting the dangers on the seas, and the importance of safeguarding France by conquering foreign territories. France allegedly had to occupy the coastal region of Algeria to eliminate the threat of pirates. During the years to come France went on to conquer all of Algeria, encountering strong resistance from Algerian warriors. After the defeat in the Franco-Prussian war of 1871, and the loss of Alsace and Lorraine, France began to encourage large-scale French settlement in Algeria.

In 1881 Tunisia became a French protectorate, under a Tunisian ruler (the "Bey"), who took direction from a French governor (a resident-general). As early as 1906, a pan-Islamic group ("Jeune Tunisiens") was founded with the explicit goal of greater national independence. Morocco was incorporated under French rule in 1912, in accordance with the same principles as Tunisia.

Already in 1887, the French introduced a naturalisation act in Algeria. The act extended French citizenship to individuals of European descent. Citizenship was not extended to the native population. In 1895, however, a new law allowed native individuals to apply for French citizenship. Since French citizenship required the abandonment of Islam, the policy was not warmly received. By 1919, "Muslims" (meaning those who were not-French citizens) were permitted to take part in representative democratic institutions in Algeria.

In the 1920s, nationalist sentiment began to escalate in North Africa. Ferhat Abbas, a moderate Algerian nationalist, argued that it was possible to be both Muslim and French. Others argued that the entire question was irrelevant since Algeria had its own culture, language and history. The path to freedom, they argued, lay in a true Islamic revival. In the interwar period, several Arab nationalistic organisations were established. In Tunisia, the Destour Party ("Constitution Party") was formed. The Party sought a modern state with universal suffrage for the Tunisian people. In 1934, Henri Bourguiba formed the Neo-Destour Party (New Constitution Party), which advocated a measured, gradual path to independence.

The 1930s witnessed multiple uprisings in North Africa as well as the establishment of numerous nationalist organisations. With the creation of the Popular Front government in France (1936), discussions on the fate of North Africa gained momentum. The Popular Front government was interested in finding alternative ways of governing the Maghreb. In 1937, Prime Minister Léon Blum proposed an extended right to vote in Algeria to Muslims to those who were not French citizens. Blum was also sympathetic to Tunisian demands for independence. But the proposal for Algeria was dropped in response to vociferous opposition from the French settlers in Algeria. In fact, this became the central dynamic in the French-Algerian relationship: Initiatives from the French government would be impeded or rejected by the settlers, and the government, reluctant to alienate this large group, would withdraw its proposals. Blum's government fell in 1938, and the Second World War broke out shortly thereafter.

During and after the war, many of the North African nationalist groups turned to the United States for support. France had been governed by the Vichy regime, under Pierre Laval, and the settlers in Algeria were, on the whole, loyal to that government. Morocco and Algeria both had been occupied by the Allies in 1940, but Tunisia had fallen to Nazi troops in 1942. The U.S. government, impressed by some of the nationalist leaders, assisted Bourguiba in his flight from Tunisia to Cairo, Egypt. And in 1943, President Roosevelt supported the Sultan of Morocco in his efforts to obtain independence. A viscerally anti-colonialist country, the United

States disliked French rule in North Africa, to the benefit of the Arab nationalists.

After the war, France made various efforts to reform its relations with Algeria. In 1947, Algeria was granted a statute that defined it as a group of provinces with its own, distinct identity. But the statute still drew a political line between French citizens and "others," i.e. those who had not abandoned Islam. As a result, Algeria was given an Algerian Assembly where half of the representatives were elected by French citizens residing in Algeria, and half by those who had not opted for French citizenship.

In Tunisia, an organised resistance against French rule took form, mainly under the direction of Bourguiba operating out of Cairo. Ferhat Abbas in Algeria contributed as well. In 1950, France's Foreign Minister Robert Schuman promised there would be reforms in Tunisia, but once again, the settlers drove a stake through these plans. With the help of right-wing parties, and the French army stationed in Tunisia, the upset frightening the French government so much so they closed the negotiations. France attempted to launch the idea of cooperative rule, but both the Tunisian people and the French settlers rejected this. Also in Morocco there were several uprisings, and also there the French settlers resisted any change in the status quo. In 1952, the question of North Africa (Tunisia and Morocco, since Algeria was now considered a part of France) found itself on the agenda of the United Nations.

Despite the fact that successive French governments had sought a looser bond with North Africa, and/or improved regulation of the democratic processes, French-North African relations in 1954 were as bad as they ever had been. The tensions cannot be attributed to the actions of only one party; the unstable parliamentary situation in France fostered fragile governments that lacked the vigour to deal effectively with the well organised and politically reactionary French settlers in North Africa. These settlers had hitherto almost single-handedly determined the fate of the Arab and Berber populations.

7.2 The year of 1954 – one step forward and two back

In 1954–1955 the situation in North Africa took a serious turn. Habib Bourguiba, the Tunisian nationalist leader, had returned to Tunisia from Cairo in 1949. The French government had in 1950 promised movement towards independence within the French Union, but confronted with strong opposition from European settlers – and from the French governor in Tunisia – the government began to relent. Bourguiba went abroad on a campaign to secure international support. Upon his return, he decided to raise the North African issue at the United Nations. French authorities detained Bourguiba in 1952, which provoked intense protests. The months to come were filled with assassinations and riots, from both sides in the conflict. When Mendès France came to power he promised to re-open the discussion on autonomy. In his much-discussed speech in Carthage on July 31, 1954, Mendès France promised autonomy for Tunisia. But it would take almost an entire year before an actual agreement was signed. In the initial stage toward autonomy, France retained control over defence and foreign policy matters. After Morocco's independence in 1956, Tunisia demanded the same. Its wish was finally granted in March 1956.

In Morocco there had been several uprisings during the early 1950s. By 1952, a serious clash seemed inevitable. Marshal Alphonse Juin, who had been governor of Morocco, strongly supported the European settlers in North Africa. Juin himself was born in Bône, in Algeria. His influence compelled the French government to force the Moroccan Sultan into exile, and bring a more 'French-minded' member of the royal family to the throne. But the deposed sultan, Mohammed V, was transformed into a nationalist hero by this event. The violence and rioting continued unabated, even after Mendès France's government came to power. Mendès France was not able to assuage the tensions in Morocco; in fact, negotiations between France and Morocco did not begin until after Mendès France's resignation, in August 1955. In December 1955, the Sultan Mohammed V returned from Madagascar to Morocco to form a new government. In March 1956 Morocco was granted independence even in foreign policy, but with cooperation with France in certain areas.

The principal conflict for France in North Africa was the Algerian War, however. Algeria, like its neighbours, had witnessed several uprisings during the first years after the Second World War. But because Algeria was much more closely tied to France, the French authorities had tighter control over the population. Since 1848, the three regions of Algeria were designated as Departments (or "administrative regions") of metropolitan France. The great Sahara-region was under military jurisdiction. In Algeria, there was also a more heterogeneous picture of nationalists than in Tunisia and Morocco, partly because the French statute for Algeria permitted some degree of representative democracy. It is not unfair to say that before 1954 it seemed as if Tunisia and Morocco would pose greater challenges to the French government than Algeria.

But this changed dramatically on November 1, 1954, the Catholic All Saints' Day. The French settlers observed this as a holy day, and were therefore utterly unprepared for what was about to take place. The many nationalist groups united under the Front de Libération Nationale (FLN) banner, and proceeded to attack French targets such as telecommunication infrastructures, military barracks, even blocking French motor traffic by erecting road barricades. This was the beginning of the Algerian War. Since this book does not aim to retell the story of Algerian War, suffice it to say that the conflict continued for more than seven years and nearly led to a military coup in France in 1958. After Charles de Gaulle had taken over the French government, subsequently becoming president, combat slowly gave way to negotiations, and finally ended in 1962 with an independent Algerian state.[171]

In July 1954, tensions in both Morocco and Tunisia were escalating. The Tunisian nationalists hoped that Mendès France would resume negotiations. Although he did engage in discussions, Mendès France spoke mainly with French representatives for settlers in Tunisia and with French party groupings there. At the Government Council of July 30, 1954, Mendès France delivered an exposé on French-Tunisian relations, promising some degree of autonomy for Tunisia. Mendès France deliberately employed the word 'autonomy' rather than 'independence'. 'Autonomy' had much the same ring as the 'self-government' that the British used.[172] Mendès France hoped for a sort of joint venture with Tunisia, where France and Tunisia would cooperate within the general framework of the French Union.

The Tunisians greeted the statement with enthusiasm. Accompanied by Marshal Juin and Christian Fouchet, the Minister for Moroccan and Tunisian affairs, Mendès France arrived in Tunis on July 31, 1954. There, he launched his idea of Tunisian self-government or 'autonomie interne'. Christian Fouchet remained in Tunis to implement the new initiative.

Nothing in the Carthage speech was new per se; Mendès France's predecessors had made similar promises But it seemed that the promises would now translate into reality. The proposal also granted universal amnesty to those who had violated rules during revolts, except for those who had committed murder. But in the French parliament, which had not been consulted before the declaration, Mendès France's actions were not greeted only with applause. One of Mendès France's adversaries, Léon Martinaud-Déplat, a prominent figure in Mendès France's own party, the Radicals, accused Mendès France of negotiating with "corrupt pirates".[173] This was of course an allusion to the French motives for conquering

---

171 For overviews and perspectives see Tricot 1972, Harmon and Rotman 1979, Talbott 1980, Joly 1991, Demker 1996, Aussaresses 2001.
172 Lacouture 1981 p. 268.
173 Lacouture 1981 p. 281.

North Africa in 1830, and therefore a extremely derogatory reference to the populations of the region. Mendès France's position was supported by the majority of the National Assembly, with 397 votes for, and 114 against.

After the Carthage speech, the march towards Tunisian independence gained momentum. In late 1955, however, conflict within the Arab nationalist groups nearly led to a French-Tunisian war. Put bluntly, the French government, now under Guy Mollet, had to choose between Algeria and Tunisia. Mollet chose Algeria and paved the path for Tunisian independence in 1956.

I have lingered on the Tunisian issue because Tunisia served as a sort 'role-model' for Morocco and Algeria. The point is obvious in the Moroccan case, since Morocco demanded independence in 1956 with direct reference to the Tunisian process. When Mendès France declared his support for Tunisian autonomy, he also could draw on the success of his approach to Indochina. As we discussed in Chapter five, Mendès France negotiated in Geneva on the basis of his conception of France, his view of national identity as something that could be chosen and was not founded on territory or history. He therefore wished for a Tunisian autonomy that would entail a general framework of cooperation with France. But he underestimated both the political strength of North Africa's French settlers and the power of nationalism among the Arabs. Undoubtedly, Mendès France's Carthage declaration was a turning point for North Africa. But maybe not of the kind he had intended or foreseen.

There can be no doubt that in Algeria, the coordinated attacks by united Algerian nationalists on the eve of All Saints' Day, 1954, was not only *a* turning point, but *the* turning point. At 6.50 a.m. on November 1, 1954, a telegram from Algiers was delivered to the Ministry of Interior in France. The telegram told of severed telephone lines, attacks against French military units, car bombs, road barricades and assaults on moving cars. The military command in Algiers requested the immediate assistance of three Special Forces Companies (CRS).[174] The troops, assisted by three battalions of paratroopers, were promptly dispatched to Algiers. The day after the initial attacks, the Arab nationalist radio (La Voix des Arabes), broadcasting from Cairo, informed its listeners that the attacks were a part of a broader plan to unite and liberate the Maghreb.[175] The Algerian Communist Party (PCA) declared on November 23 that Algeria is "notre pays" (our country) and demanded independence.[176] Soon after, Algerian mayors (mainly Europeans) requested that the Algerian Communist Party

---

[174] Telegramme Nov 1, 1954. Dossier "Algèrie", Vol I.
[175] Note le directeur de cabinet, Nov 1954, Dossier "Algèrie", Vol I.
[176] Declaration, Nov 23, 1954, Dossier "Algèrie", Vol I.

be prohibited, that the "terrorists" be arrested, and that the Algerian parliamentarians protested against the French government in Paris.[177] The walls were built immediately.

French policy towards North Africa had been in the shadows of the war in Indochina for quite a long time. It was not only that Indochina received more attention because it was an international conflict; it was also a territory to which French opinion felt somehow less connected. North Africa struck a far more emotional chord. After the fall of Dien Bien Phu, the French military could not come up with strong enough arguments to convince France to keep Indochina French. Indeed, French opinion welcomed the end of the Indochina War. But Algeria was different. It stood out even from the other North African countries. I will therefore concentrate on the beginning of the Algerian War and on Mendès France's actions during that first phase. In next section of the chapter, I also discuss the spring of 1956, when Mendès France – as a member of Mollet's government and therefore an important actor in the Algerian drama resigned from his post in Mollet's government

In the years immediately following the Second World War, the population in Algeria underwent some important changes. The following figures help illustrate the structural force of matters such as population density and distribution of land. The European population – i.e. those of European descent – stood at about 1 000 000; but the Moslem population had increased at a much higher rate, and in the year of 1954 stood at about 8 500 000. About 90 per cent of the Moslem population was illiterate.[178] Only a limited number of individuals of Moslem background had the privilege of higher education. In 1954 there were, for example, 165 males of Moslem heritage in the medical profession.[179] Another revealing discrepancy was in the allocation of land. In 1951, some 440 000 Moslem farms (which amounted to 70 per cent of Moslem-owned agricultural land) had less than ten hectares to cultivate. Only 35 percent of the Europeans, or 7 500 individuals in total, were in that same position. Only 1.5 per cent of Moslem farmers (8 500 farmers) had more than 100 hectares to cultivate, while 30 per cent of the Europeans, or 6 500 persons, enjoyed such amounts. It is important to remember that most of the Europeans were employed in industry, commerce or the liberal professions (lawyers, physicians and others).[180]

177 Declaration, not dated, Dossier "Algérie", Vol I.
178 Clayton 1994, p. 108.
179 Clayton 1994, p. 109.
180 Mémo about the Algerian population 1948 and 1951, Dossier "Algérie", Vol XI.

The coastal cities were dominated by the Europeans before the Second World War, but in 1954, two-thirds of the urban population was comprised of Algerian Moslems. But as time passed, many of the so-called Europeans became Algerians. Persons like the author Albert Camus, who was of European descent but born and raised in Algeria, saw Algeria as their homeland. Europeans in Algeria could no longer readily be classified as "Frenchmen abroad". Like the Moslem Algerians, these individuals had no other home than Algeria. This was to be the stickiest question for Mendès France, as it had been for so many European colonial powers with settlers in Africa. Mendès France refused to accept that these two self-defined groups of Algerian populations were in fact two groups. His views were not shared by many in the French foreign policy elite.

When the right to vote was extended in Tunisia and Morocco in 1955, citizens were officially classified into the following groups: French, including naturalized Moslems; other Europeans; Moslem Tunisians; Tunisian Jews; French Moslems from Algeria; foreign Moslems; and Jewish Tunisians.[181] Mendès France found such categorisations unacceptable. In his speech before the executive committee of the Radical Party on April 20, 1956, he speaks of "la population algérienne" (the Algerian *population*) instead of "les populations algériennes" (the Algerian *populations*). But when the executive committee began to formulate its communiqué on the meeting, members demanded that the term "les populations algériennes" be used. Mendès France acquiesced. He resisted, however, the demand to include the concept "l'intégrité du territoire de la République Française" ("The integrity of the territory of the French Republic"), a phrase that affirmed that Algeria was a part of France. The new concept of "l'intégrité de l'Algérie Française" (integrity of French Algeria) was introduced instead. Mendès France was enraged, and rejected this formulation as well. The term expressed an extreme and conservative conception of an Algeria headed by Europeans.[182]

The main strategy for Mendès France was to hold the nationalists back via military means, while simultaneously implementing political and social reforms so that all Algerians could benefit from economic development. He envisioned a French Union where countries would cooperate with one another, but where association with France was a guarantee for collective social goods. It was the question of reforms that would give Mendès France the most trouble.

181 A Jordan to A Pélabon, mémo, January 1955, Dossier "Algérie", Vol IV.
182 Protocol, PR Executive committee, April 20, 1956. Dossier Pierre Mendès France vol L'Afrique du Nord/Gouvernment Guy Mollet.

In the beginning of the War, France had ample troops to dispatch to the front. Around new-year 1955, there were 25 000 French soldiers and policemen in Algeria. But the implementation of already existing laws, and the acceptance of new reforms, was very slow. Directly after the outbreak of the revolt, some 100 teachers and middle-class Europeans drafted an "open letter" to Mendès France. They demanded an end to the violence, and asked that the French principles of humanitarianism, which they taught and were taught in school, be adhered to by France itself. They argued that separating state and religion, along with extensive education in Arabic, would constitute the first step towards "la construction de l'Algérie de demain, dans laquelle chacun aura sa place" (the construction of an Algeria of tomorrow, where everyone has a place").[183]

Georges Bourdat, who worked on North African issues in Mendès France's Prime Ministerial cabinet, advised the director of the cabinet, André Pélabon, that "la meilleure manière d'aider les familles algérienne me semble être d'assurer une scolarisation satisfiante de leurs enfants" ("the best way to assist Algerian families is to assure their children of an adequate education."). It was through this, he argued, that the Algerian people could gain a place in the French community.[184] It is obvious that the low level of education among the Moslem population was recognized as a problem – both by those who resided in Algeria, and those who were in the position to govern.

There had been several attempts to bring about the full integration of Algeria with France, in more than the administrative sense. Already in March 1953 – more than one year before the Mendès France government – Georges Bourdat discussed ways in which to integrate Algeria into the broader European community. Bourdat authored a report that was sent to the French government by the Algerian governor Roger Léonard. Bourdat listed four possible solutions to the Algeria question, along with his thoughts on each: 1. A "Eurafrica" – not advisable, purely colonialist; 2. the entire French Union gaining a place in the emerging European community – unrealistic; 3. only the French republic inside the European community, with Algeria either divided or sliding toward independence; or 4. only the European part of France inside the European community, with Algeria as a part of DOM-TOM (territories outside Europe with a special position in the French constitution) and movement towards independence. Léonard noted that according to the formulations

183 Document, November 1954, Dossier "Algerie" Vol I.
184 Letter Bourdat to Pélabon, Octobre 25, 1954. Dossier "Algérie", Vol II.

of the French constitution (as it stood in 1953), Algeria would enter the European community along with France.[185]

My conclusion, after reviewing the governmental files on Algeria during the years 1953–1954, is that there were several serious and realistic plans and reforms proposed for Algeria. The problem was that they did not gain the acceptance of the European settlers, of the Conservative opposition and/or of the French administration in Algeria. Those who wanted reforms were naturalised French citizens in Algeria, assimilated Moslems, an educated European middle class, intellectuals in France and Algeria, and several liberal and radical party groups on both sides of the Mediterranean. All of these sides ended up as losers when the war broke out in Algeria: Algerian residents of French descent were suddenly forced to a life in a European country of which they knew virtually nothing, while Algerian Moslems were forced to take a stand for an Arabic nationalism that demanded they cut ties with France and all French culture. Albert Camus was one of the Europeans, born and raised in Algeria, who refused to take a stand; in his literary legacy, he has left us with profound insights about what is lost when we are forced to choose between two evils.

The reforms that François Mitterrand, then-Minister of the Interior, sought to introduce in autumn 1954 were not focused on issues such as the lack of education, despite widespread recognition of the problem. Instead, the reform plan indicated the desire to forcibly implement the Algerian Statute of 1947. In his explanation for the reforms, the term "la communauté franco-musulmane" (the French-Moslem community) was employed. The choice of terms indicates a minor weight in favour of the view of Algeria as populated by several 'populations'. A new categorisation of regions was introduced to facilitate contact between administration and the populations. Several regions were transformed into genuine French administrative communities, voting rights for Moslem women were introduced, and a new inter-ministerial committee for North Africa appointed.

The reforms were conducted with the explicit motive of "poursuivre progressivement l'oeuvre d'intégration complète de l'Algérie à la communauté Française" (progressively move toward the complete integration of Algeria into the French community).[186] But as had been the case for several years, certain power-holders in Algeria opposed the reforms. This time it was the French governor (General Roger Léonard) of Algeria who most adamantly rejected the idea. Mitterrand wrote to Mendès France, asking

---

185 File about social and economic status in Algeria until summer 1954, mémo Bourdat/Léonard March, 27, 1953. Dossier "Algerie", Vol III.

186 Mémo Min of interior, F Mitterrand, January 3, 1955. Dossier "Algerie", Vol II.

that he replace Léonard with someone more interested in political reform. Mitterrand noted the difficulties in working with someone in Algeria who would "dire non aux excès, aux mensonges, aux abus, aux fanatismes" and simultaneously "s'identifié à la pérennité de la France en Afrique du Nord" ("say no to excesses, lies, abuses, and fanaticism, and – at the same time – identifies with France as some eternal force in North Africa.)[187] In December 1954, the French parties "les Indépendants" and "les Paysans" (both conservative parties) criticized the government's North Africa policy at their party congresses.[188] The reforms in Algeria were meant to pose a serious challenge to the nationalists, but because they failed to address what was perceived as the greatest problem (education), and because of obstruction from the administration in Algeria, the reforms did not have the desired effects.

Mendès France most likely understood that North Africa would be too great of a problem. He nearly lost a vote in the National Assembly in November 1954. With a majority of only 40 votes, Mendès France obtained support for his Algerian – and broader North Africa – policy. On December 10, it was again time for the National Assembly to vote, this time on the autonomy of Morocco and Tunisia. Mendès France's policy passed with a majority of just 29 votes. This was the narrowest margin yet for the Mendès France government. Most members of the MRP (Christian democrats) opposed him; the Conservatives generally voted against; the socialists voted in favour; and his own Radical party was divided. During the winter of 1954–55, numerous difficult issues, such as the Paris Accords over the relations to Germany, were being negotiated. The records indicate that Mendès France did not concentrate his best efforts on the Algeria question. His inability to manage the revolts in Algeria revealed the weakness of his position. He was lambasted for having brought about the revolts in Algeria by granting Tunisia autonomy. In his defence, Mendès France reminded his colleagues that "dix gouvernements" had promised autonomy to Tunisia, and that it was high time these promises were fulfilled, yet this argument failed to persuade his adversaries.[189]

In February 1955 Mendès France was again faced with a debate on North Africa. He had replaced Léonard with Jacques Soustelle as governor of Algeria. Soustelle was unpopular among the European population of Algeria. René Mayer, leading the opposition, accused Mendès France of "conduire à la secession ou à l'exode de Français d'origine européenne"

---

187 Letter Mitterrand to Mendès France, January 19, 1955. Dossier "Algérie", Vol II.
188 "L'Information" December 9, 1954. Dossier "Algerie", Vol III.
189 *L'Année politique* 1954, p. 104.

(bringing about secession, or an exodus of the French of European descent in Algeria).[190] None of the arguments presented by, for example Christian Fouchet, who directed the implementation of Tunisian autonomy, could calm the debate.

Mendès France entered the platform and attempted to justify his position on North Africa. He spoke about "l'Afrique du Nord" (North Africa), while Mayer had chosen to talk of populations, Europeans, and the Algerian problem. The difference in terms was no coincidence: It should be interpreted as deliberate choice on the part of Mendès France. It is clear from archival documentation that Mendès France was highly conscious of his words. It is reasonable to interpret his avoidance of the term "Algerian" as being quite deliberate. Mendès France had quite another perspective than Mayer and others on the issue, a perspective where European France was more or less detached from North Africa. North Africa was for him a territory, a territory that was administered by and from France, but not – as for Mayer – *a part of* France. Mendès France defended his belief in a policy that valued reform rather than force. François Mitterrand also defended the government's chosen policy, arguing that the implementation of reforms was a necessary strategy, while still underlining that France should remain in North Africa.[191]

Mendès France lost this vote by a margin of 46 votes. It was mainly the MRP (Christian-democrats) that had switched sides. Support came from the Socialists, the Radicals and the Republicans – all left-liberal groupings – while the conservative groups voted against him.

In February 1955 Mendès France's actions in North Africa reached their end. Autonomy in Tunisia represented a step forward, or at least was seen as such in North Africa. But the war in Algeria undoubtedly represented two steps back for both parts. Mendès France was to return, but not until one year later. In this first phase, the turning points were the Carthage-declaration (July 31, 1954), and the unsuccessful implementation of the Mitterrand reform plan. It is also worth noting that Mendès France had very little time to devote to the North Africa issue when the revolts first erupted in Algeria. His main political focus during the autumn 1954 was – besides Indochina – the question of Germany as negotiated in the Paris Accords in October, and disarmament talks within the framework of the United Nations.

---

190 *L'Année politique* 1955, p. 12.
191 *L'Année politique* 1955, p. 13.

7.3 The year of 1956 – steps along another pathway

Over the course of 1955, Pierre Mendès France continued to oppose France's North Africa policy, especially as it pertained to Algeria. In June, Tunisia took the first step towards independence by signing the protocol that recognized Tunisian autonomy. Habib Bourguiba made a direct reference to Algeria: He noted that it would seem peculiar for Morocco and Tunisia to be independent, while Algeria, in between the two, remained "under the colonialist yoke".[192] But despite Soustelle's efforts, no genuine reforms were introduced in Algeria. Efforts to implement reforms were deliberately obstructed by the European dominated Assembly in Algeria.[193] Soustelle found himself in a deepening morass; he attempted a dialogue with moderate nationalists, but was greeted only with suspicion by both European settlers and the more radical Arab nationalists.[194] He therefore never "dared offer any acceptable solution," in the words of Anthony Clayton.[195]

A committee for North African affairs was established in June 1955 to support Prime Minister Edgar Faure, with Marshal Juin and General Koenig among its members.[196] In March 1955, France declared a state of emergency. In August, the National Assembly extended this state, and also stipulated a new administrative region (a fourth Department) as well the reorganisation of the judicial system with the creation of two new courts of appeal. At the same time, the French government was sending enormous military contingents to Algeria. In the summer of 1955 there were more than 100 000 French soldiers in Algeria. Eventually, this number would reach over 400 000 (in 1957).[197] Camps for the detention of violent nationalists were established in 1955, and military trials were conducted in Algeria with the full sanction of the French government.[198] The summer of 1955 witnessed several attacks and massacres in Algeria. On, August 20, 1955, some 71 Europeans and 61 Moslems loyal to the French regime were killed. The French response was horrifying: about 3 000 people were gunned down by both French soldiers and European settlers.[199]

---

192 *Time Magazine*, April 2, 1956.
193 Clayton 1994, p. 118.
194 Soustelle tried to accomplish an "intégration" in French Algeria, to resist the decolonisation. This policy was founded on the idea of eternal bonds between France and Algeria. Tyre 2006.
195 Clayton 1994, p. 117.
196 *L'Année politique* 1955, p. 51.
197 Chamberlain 1998, p. 161.
198 Clayton 1994, p. 117.
199 Clayton 1994, p. 118–119.

Amid all of this horror, in letters directly to the French government, the International Red Cross deplored the fact that it was denied access to camps and prisons. Several letters were sent, some with unequivocal indictments of France for retaining people in custody without trial. The International Red Cross demanded that it be permitted to visit police stations, implying that it believed torture was being used by the French.[200]

French politicians did travel to Algeria during the summer of 1955. The Minister of the Interior, Maurice Bourges-Manoury, and a group of parliamentarians, including the Socialist and former Nazi camp prisoner Christian Pineau, visited Algeria and drafted reports on what they found. Bourges-Manoury wrote to the Minister of Defence (General Koenig), insisting that it was more important than ever to demonstrate French willingness to integrate Algeria into the French national territory. He also appealed for symbolic measures that would take into account religious sentiment among the Moslem population. Bourges-Manoury suggested, for instance, that France open a military school in Algeria. A greater number of Moslems would thus develop an interest in a military career, laying excellent foundations for a new sort of Algerian elite, he argued.[201] Mendès France had made the same suggestion in December 1954, at no avail.[202]

Christian Pineau's report painted quite a different picture. Pineau was concerned about the fact that the French administration in Algeria "semble avoir perdu progressivement depuis dix ans, le contact avec une grande partie des populations musulmans." (seems to have lost, progressively over the past ten years, contact with a large part of the Moslem populations.) Pineau feared that the military force should be allowed to work on its own in Algeria. He underlined that the "justice et la force, la seconde au service de la première sont, pour le moment, les deux seuls atouts de la France en Algérie" (justice and force, the second at the service of the first, are for the moment, the two only cards that France has to play in Algeria.)[203] There is a sort of double-meaning in Pineau's statements. On the one hand, Pineau described the situation as he saw it and as he believed it had to be, but the underlying tone of the report is one of genuine sorrow over this state of affairs. It is impossible to read Pineau's report without concluding that he deeply regretted the impasse between France and Algeria.

The war only escalated during autumn 1955, and the Faure government

200 Exchange of letters, mémo, May 23, 1955. Dossier "Algérie", Vol III.
201 Report, From Bourges-Manoury to Defence Ministry, July 7, 1955. Dossier "Algerie", Vol IV.
202 Letter from Mendès France to Defence Ministry, December 10, 1954. Dossier "Algérie", Vol IV.
203 Report Pineau, July 5, 1955. Travel took place June 4–9, 1955. Dossier "Algérie", Vol IV.

fell at last in November. Ordinary parliamentary elections were held in January 1956. The Socialist party, led by Guy Mollet, managed to form a government, and Mendès France chose to join as Minister without Portfolio. His former Chief of the Prime Minister's staff, André Pélabon, appealed to him to take on the Algerian issue and attempt to become Prime Minister.[204] But Mendès France rejected the proposition, arguing that Guy Mollet was "moins mal accueilli" (less poorly viewed) than himself. Mendès France also underlined that it was not desirable to be in charge of policy towards Algeria and Prime Minister at the same time.[205]

There were two developments that would have a major impact in the Algerian question. First, Soustelle was replaced as governor in Algeria (Robert Lacoste) and second, Guy Mollet visited Algeria himself. Lacoste was a "conservative hard-liner".[206] And he was appointed when the European settlers categorically rejected the first candidate – Georges Catroux. Responding to their protests, Mollet removed Catroux. The replacement clearly indicated the level of influence enjoyed by the European settlers over the French government. As a consequence, Lacoste was less of a representative of the French government to Algeria, and more of a representative of the European settlers to the French government.

Mollet appeared deeply moved by his visit to Algeria. Upon his return, he spoke before the National Assembly about the experience. In what became a turning point in French North Africa policy, Mollet declared that he was convinced that "la grande masse des Européens n'est pas prête à suivre les extrémistes. (...) Hors d'Algérie, ils ne peuvent vivre." (The great majority of the Europeans are not ready to follow the extremists. (...) Outside of Algeria, they cannot live.) Mollet thus did not believe that the Europeans in Algeria were inclined to follow the groups that demanded more forceful policy against the FLN. In fact, it seemed that these Europeans really were Algerians. While he spoke of Algeria as the homeland of the European settlers, however, Mollet also distinguished that group from "l'immense masse musulmane" (the enormous Moslem masses). Algeria clearly was the homeland also for them, but Mollet rejected the conflicting national identities implied by talking about both the European settlers and the Moslem population as Algerians. Mollet tried to circumvent the issue by referring to "la personnalité algérienne" ("the Algerian personality.) But this Algerian personality was not determined by only one party, he argued. Mollet wished to create "une communauté franco-musulmane

---

204 Letter from Pélabon to Mendès France, January 23, 1956. Dossier "Algerie", Vol IV.
205 Letter from Mendès France to Pélabon, January 26, 1956. Dossier "Algerie", Vol IV.
206 Chamberlain 1998 p. 161.

fraternelle".[207] In a radio speech some days later, Mollet again discussed "the Algerian personality." He repeatedly employed phrases such as "la collectivité musulmane", "Algériens d'origine européenne", and "Les musulmans d'Algerie" (the Moslem collective, Algerian of European origin, and Moslems of Algeria).[208] The perspective expressed by Mollet was markedly different from that of Mendès France. Mendès France usually spoke about "Algériens musulmans" and "Algériens européennes" (Algerian Moslems, Algerian Europeans). By this, he avoided defining the populations as having conflicting national identities. Mendès France could therefore speak about all Algerians as having common national identity founded on their factual status in the country. Mollet instead chose to describe the Algerian population as composed of two distinct groups, where one had the right to make claims for special treatment because of its European heritage.

By the spring of 1956 the French government was clearly divided over the Algeria question. Mollet ordered a massive transfer of troops to Algeria, and conscription was introduced. Mendès France criticized Lacoste's plan for reforms, leading to a deep cleavage between the two. His criticism of Lacoste was that the timing of the reforms was had been ill conceived and that military force and agricultural reforms should have been implemented simultaneously.[209] Already in April 1956, Mendès France began to discuss whether he should resign. On April 21, Mendès France wrote a letter to Mollet with several proposals for a new policy on Algeria. This policy was by no means revolutionary, and appeared carefully thought out. The main theme of the proposals was that any successful solution to the Algeria question had to be political, rather than military. Mendès France argued that France needed to create a climate in which negotiations could take place, and should begin by liberating prisoners, expropriating large estates, dissolving local assemblies (which only used their power to obstruct governmental reforms) and plan for negotiations with the nationalist groups. Mendès France's advisors did not believe that Mollet would embrace these proposals; yet Mollet's government was Socialist, and the propositions were all compatible with Socialist ideology. It should therefore have been possible for Mendès France's ideas to be accepted.[210]

207 Mollet; Speech in the Assemblé Nationale, February 16, 1956.
208 Manuscript, Radio speech February 28, 1956, Guy Mollet. Dossier "Algérie", Vol VIII.
209 Letter Mendès France to Lacoste, april 5, 1956; Letter Bourdat to Mendès France May 22, 1956; Article by Mendès France in "Combat" april 12, 1956. Dossier Pierre Mendès France vol l'Afrique du Nord/Gouvernement Guy Mollet.
210 Letter from René Lacharrière to Mendès France, April 7. 1956. Dossier Pierre Mendès France vol l'Afrique du Nord/Gouvernement Guy Mollet; Undated Mémo, 1956, plan for negotiations with the FLN (possible by Georges Bourdat). Dossier "Algérie", Vol XI.

Yet they were not. It was this that led directly to Mendès France's resignation on May 23, 1956. Mendès France never returned to the French government, although he remained politically active in the Algerian issue during the entire war. His letter of resignation was as much a policy statement as a resignation. George Boris and Jean-Jacques Servan-Schreiber had written several drafts for the letter.[211] In it, Mendès France argued that the escalation of the war would eventually lead to the abandonment of Algeria, and eventually of all of Africa. Mollet had stated repeatedly that France never would abandon Algeria.[212]

By accepting a ministerial role that was neither the Prime Minister nor a position focused on Algeria, Mendès France limited his own political influence and power. His views on policy towards North Africa were different than most of his colleagues– and without a strong power base, he could not convince them of his views. This was, in a sense, a turning point. The appointment of Robert Lacoste was a turning point in the true sense: From that day forward, Mendès France's influence declined markedly. The European settlers had learned that it was they who exercised power. It was in deference to them that Mollet had exchanged Catroux for Lacoste. And, unlike Soustelle, Lacoste did not share the views of Mendès France. Mendès France thus found himself trapped, almost held hostage inside a government whose policies he opposed and whom he could not influence.

7.4 Conclusions

On the surface, Mendès France's failure in North Africa could easily be explained by the lack of time devoted to the question during the first important phase, or by the decline in political support for Mendès France's Radical Party. A different picture has emerged in this Chapter, however. I have emphasised that Mendès France's discourse about North Africa could not have been accepted because it was founded on national identity conceptions that were not supported by power holders in French society at that time. For them Algeria was a part of France; French Algeria existed, not Algeria. In the Indochina War, the French military was proven too weak, and could not persuade the government of the importance of keeping Indochina "French." In addition, there were far fewer European settlers in Indochina than in North Africa, and they did not act as a unified

---

211 There are seven drafts from J-J Servan-Schreiber and some comments from G Boris.
Dossier Pierre Mendès France vol Afrique du Nord/Gouvernement Guy Mollet.
212 Lacouture 1986, p. 423.

political force. In North Africa, the French military were power-holders, in part because they administrated vast territories, but also because they were supported by well organised political forces in North Africa.

The Europeans in North Africa were – mainly by administrative regulations – part of the French party system. Because of this they had easier access to the National Assembly and other representative institutions in metropolitan France. None of these power-holders shared Mendès France's conception of national identity. And Mendès France did not succeed in stretching – or extending – the discourse, as he had in Indochina.

Let us take a closer look at the political process. Soon after the Geneva Accords that ended the Indochina War, Mendès France expressed his views on French relations with North Africa in his speech in Carthage. It is clear that this speech was seen as a sort of 'model' for all three Maghreb-countries, both by Mendès France and by the nationalist leaders in North Africa. In the speech, or statement, Mendès France highlights that trustful relations will lead to autonomy and cooperation within a loosely organised framework, the French Union. For Mendès France, national identity was not bound to a territory or to history, but to the willingness to cooperate for a common goal. It is obvious that Mendès France underestimated the power of other conceptions.

The Carthage speech was the first turning point in the process. The statement made there opened up both for the criticism of policy in place as being weak and support for independence.

What happened afterwards was decisive. When the Algerian revolt erupted in November 1954, Mendès France seemed unable to respond. He was physically absent at the time (he was on a visit to Canada) and he seemed quite surprised by the coordination, organisation and strategic focus of the revolt. Despite the fact that there were many efforts to regulate relations between Algeria and France in a more constructive and positive manner, and despite that the conflict had been escalating since 1945, Mendès France had no other answer than military force and further reforms. When French troops begun to be dispatched, Mendès France had taken his first step on the same road favoured by most others: that of force and oppression. This could not be smoothed over by further reform plans. The inability to implement the Mitterrand plan was the explicit and overt sign of the coming failure. It was a sign of weakness in the eyes of Mendès France's adversaries.

The incidents in November 1954 could have been a turning point in favour of Mendès France's policies, had he effectively used the opportunity. But he had several complex issues before him, including that of relations with Germany, which he prioritised. This can be seen as a missed opportunity that was decisive to the future of Mendès France's policies on North Africa. That he did not resign immediately was due more to his personal popularity and the lack of attractive alternatives, than to his policies.

When Mendès France returned in 1956, he assumed a governmental position that provided him with neither influence on the Algerian policy nor legitimacy to disengage from that issue. Instead, he accepted a post 'in-between'. He thus left the door open for Guy Mollet's harsher policy, and created potential fissures within the government. This can be considered a turning point away from Mendès France's objectives. Mollet's exchange of Soustelle with Lacoste, after having accepted the protests over Catroux, marked the second turning point in this phase. Mollet had had his "eyes opened" to the situation for the European settlers in Algeria, and his visit there was a watershed in his policy. He began a policy of intense repression of the FLN by military means, and a number of accounts note that it was under Mollet's tenure that the French began to use torture in the war.

As governor of Algeria, Soustelle had indeed turned away from Mendès France's ideas about Algeria, but he was still more in agreement with Mendès France's visions than Lacoste ever would be. Lacoste was a conservative who mainly shared the visions of the European settlers; he wished to keep Algeria French, but in the conventional, territorial sense. Lacoste also preferred a strategy that would roll back the FLN before the reforms were implemented. For Mendès France these things would have taken place in just the opposite sequence. The conflict between Lacoste and Mendès France directly led to Mendès France's resignation in May 1956, although his conflict was as much with Mollet as it was with Lacoste. The appointment of Lacoste confirmed that the European settlers had a strong power base and could influence the French government, and it signalled that the phase of politically progressive reforms in Algeria was over.

To summarise, the Tunisian model (Carthage-speech) and the missed opportunity in the outbreak of the revolt in Algeria were the turning points in the first phase. The unwillingness to take full responsibility for policy towards North Africa, or to assume a post that would entirely disengage him from that question, together with the circumstances around the appointment of Lacoste as governor in Algeria, were the two turning points in the second phase.

The failure of Pierre Mendès France's North Africa policy was the consequence of a conflict between his identity conceptions and the identity conceptions of the European settlers and the French military establishment. In the Indochina case, Mendès France was able to focus other parties on a solution, despite differing motives. In the case of North Africa, he was unable to overcome the schism between identity conceptions. The reason for this was the lack of power of these conceptions. The French military had regained its power after having been humiliated in Indochina, and was keen on restoring its honour after that debacle.

The European settlers in their turn recognized that they could exercise power over French political parties and the government because of the identity crisis and a weak executive. Mendès France's identity conceptions were not compatible with the discourse on North Africa, and they were not supported by a power base. In the Indochina case this was of no consequence. Mendès France was able to temporarily stretch the discourse, because the power bases were either eroding (military) or unorganised (settlers). But in North Africa this was not the case. There, Mendès France was a victim of the discourse.

8.
National Identity, Discourse and Power

A brief summary of my central findings from my study of Pierre Mendès France and his efforts to solve the conflicts in Indochina and North Africa is: That his conception of France – which was also the foundation of his policy – differed from the common conception and was not compatible with the power structures in French society. That the prevalent identity conception at the time emphasized the historical legacy of France as a nation-state with an empire, and also rested on geographical and social foundations. That Mendès France's conception of France, however, was founded on political values such as economic growth and progress, social cooperation, and justice. And that the French identity discourse was too empowered and rigid to be altered by the efforts of a single individual, despite Mendès France's position of leadership.

The answer to why Mendès France succeeded in Indochina, but failed in North Africa, is thus as follows: In the Indochina case, Mendès France's conception of France never challenged prevailing French power structures, which were reproduced through the identity discourse in place in France. The solution to the Indochina conflict was compatible with the perimeters of the discourse. In the case of North Africa, however, Mendès France's conception was irreconcilable with the prevailing identity discourse; his conception profoundly challenged – not reproduced – its very foundations.

In this concluding chapter, my intention is not only to summarise my findings, but also to take the discussion about identity-explanations further and propose a discursive concept of national identity and a hypothesis about when and how national identity conceptions can be transformed.[213] I believe that my study provides support for a perspective that differs from those normally associated with constructivist research.

8.1 Why did Mendès France succeed in Indochina but fail in Algeria?

In most literature on political change, it is said that periods of crisis provide the opportunity for the introduction of new ideas.[214] In my study of France in 1953–1955, I have therefore tried first to establish whether France did indeed experience an identity crisis during these years. Was there an opportunity for a new identity to be successfully introduced and adopted? After analysing media debates, political actions and parliamentary relations in France, my answer is that France undeniably did experience an identity crisis. At the argument level, the identity crisis was manifested most obviously through vague self-perceptions and nebulous definitions of the boundaries of the national community. National values were less discussed. On the discourse level, we find the reverse, namely, that national values were vague or polarised, but the self-perception was clearly expressed in the divide between the people and the establishment. The borders of the national community were as confusing as they appeared to be at the argument level. Finally, on the foundational level the identity crisis was expressed in a debate about what "we" stood for, i.e. a colonial power or the working class, and where 'being French' could be defined on a cultural, class, or territorial basis. Values, however, were mainly universal in nature and inclusive, and were not debated. It is therefore clear that France experienced an identity crisis during 1953–1955, suggesting that the conditions for the transformation of national identity were there. If Mendès France had a distinct identity conception, one that differed from earlier conceptions, it should have been possible to introduce this vision as a new foundation for foreign policy.

Assessing Mendès France's network, it becomes evident that also in the narrowest of circles, Mendès France was a solitary figure. His conception of France differed from that of almost everyone else in the foreign policy elite, adversaries as well as friends. Yet there was no clear consensus about French identity in the foreign policy elite. A lack of true power in the

---

213 A 'discursive concept' is a step-by-step-definition, unlike an essential or stipulated concept with distinct criteria.
214 Checkel 1997a, Ringmar 1996, Finnemore & Sikkink 2001:405–406.

political system allowed room for other groups to influence the political decision-making process. Economic interest groups, the military, and various extremist groupings thus were important actors in shaping French identity.

What, then, was Mendès France's identity conception of France? His view of France differed from the prevailing view, putting a greater emphasis on 'political' dimensions. Mendès France emphasized the political system and the people's closeness to, and support for, that system as the main goal, cause and value of national identity. In this study, I therefore have maintained that for Mendès France, the self-perception of France centred on political institutions and citizenship. The focus was not on territorial or ethnic boundaries, but on an value-based attachment to the political institutions of France. Accordingly, Mendès France's interpretation of "national community" underlined self-selection: Those who wished to be on the inside, and who remained loyal to the political institutions of France, would, in the political process, create a community defined by common objectives and solidarity. Mendès France also believed that national values rested on universal principles such as progress, autonomy, development and justice. His conception of France also was anchored in material and economic resources. He maintained that France was only as strong as her ability to reform, develop and progress. A nation's 'grandeur,' according to Mendès France, was concealed in its future. Therefore, a nation's ability to develop and to generate economic growth was more important than history in defining the nation. Mendès France thus drew on an economic and rational world view that was alien to many of his counterparts and colleagues.

The two case studies employed in this study, Indochina and North Africa, support the contention that Mendès France managed to negotiate and reach a broadly accepted solution for Indochina because his assumptions about France did not challenge the identity conception of existing basic power structures. The relationship between Indochina and France never included a sense of territorial unity. In addition, the military seemed impotent, failing utterly to defend French identity in Indochina. In discussions on North Africa, particularly in regards to Algeria, Mendès France challenged powerful identity conceptions held by several important groups in France. And the military had not yet failed in its defence of French interests in Algeria as it had in Indochina. Significant groups within Mendès France's immediate entourage held the notion that Algeria was a part of France. Mendès France failed in his effort to change or expand the notions of French identity, despite the evident identity crisis experienced by France at the time. According to much of the literature on identity crises, this moment in history should have been a golden opportunity to transform national identity. Instead, my study concludes that during times of identity crisis, older or more commonly accepted identities can actually gain ground, preventing the emergence of new identities. My thesis, on the basis of this study, is that the chances of introducing and gaining acceptance for a new national identity in a democracy are in reality far slimmer during times of crisis than during periods of stability.

The case studies show that the French military on the one hand, and the deep ideological cleavages between parties and groupings on the other, represented the power relations that determined the discourse on national identity. This discourse was sufficiently broad to include several different arguments, however, and Mendès France's position did not challenge the foundations of the identity. But when Mendès France attempted to alter the discourse, the very way in which national identity was discussed, he challenged the foundations of the prevailing French identity. The military still enjoyed a great deal of power, largely due to the political system's loss of authority. The struggle between parties and the parliament, with extremists on both sides challenging the system as a whole, produced a discourse about national identity that allowed no room for Mendès France's conception of France. He failed to expand the discourse, despite his efforts during the Indochina-negotiations, because he chose to work outside of these existing power relations. His decision to do so was deliberate, in part driven by his belief that his direct appeals to the French people through media (radio, newspapers), and his clear and outspoken political style would be sufficiently powerful and persuasive. He failed to recognize how powerful the current discourse on French identity was.

Could he have acted differently? This is of course a counter-factual argument, but we know that Charles de Gaulle, without any of the old parties behind him, managed to change – or at least somewhat shift – the conception of France.[215] He preserved the notion of France as a global power, but shifted the emphasis from the colonial empire to the European arena. We also know that both the French political system and military power were broken in the coup of 1958. In light of this, perhaps it would have been possible for Mendès France to change French identity conception. He had, after all, served Free France and de Gaulle during the Second World War, and was a well-known politician, a moderate on the ideological spectrum who enjoyed great popular support. In other words, he had

---

215 De Gaulle did manage to "use" a political crisis, mostly because the power structures (military, political parties) had shown there impotence.

the proper qualifications: he had resisted the Nazis; he covered a broad ideological base and held a democratic, legitimate position for influencing the political landscape in France. On the other hand, it could be argued that his moderate stance prevented him from effectively dealing with the extremists on both sides of the political spectrum, and that he lacked the experience of military leadership. From the military perspective he thus was not a legitimate leader, and he lacked organisational support since his party soon found itself divided. In a sense, we can borrow from Mendès France's own words, cited in Chapter One, and say that he was useful in paving the way for de Gaulle. De Gaulle was the man that, given Mendès France belief in historical determinism, found exactly the right moment in which to act.

8.2 National identity – a discursive order

In this study I have advocated a theoretical perspective on national identity that can be described as constructivist. Constructivism is a theoretical approach that argues that our social world is the manifestation of our common understanding. Concepts such as ideas, norms and discourse are central to constructing knowledge about our world. The constructivist approach was introduced to the discipline of International Politics in the 1980s, but it rests on much older scientific suppositions. Reacting to the idea that it was possible to 'observe', 'investigate' and 'analyse' the world, a group of philosophers proposed a new, interpretative way of understanding the world. In their quest, they were strongly influenced by the hermeneutic approach that had been used during 19th century efforts to translate and interpret the Bible. Positivism emerged in Vienna in the 1920s, with its emphasis on scientific accuracy and rigor, prompting the "interpretivists" to increasingly refine their own approach. Edmund Husserl, Martin Heidegger, Hans-Georg Gadamer and Georg Lukács were among the most important early interpretivists. American pragmatism, led by Charles Saunders Pierce, William James and Wilhelm Dilthey, also was influential.[216] During this time, the fundamental insight that social relations are not a fixed reality, but rather are constantly constructed, shaped, and reshaped, evolved into foundation for subsequent theoretical perspectives and emerging scientific methods. For the past 35 years, the

---

[216] For a discussion of a modern influential constructivist path, namely neo-pragmatism, see Reitberger 2000.

constructivist perspective has been a more or less accepted approach in the social sciences.[217]

Identity is not, I have argued in this book, an inherent property, or reducible to individual opinions and attitudes. In accordance with the constructivist nature of national identity, I treated the concept in my analysis of French decolonisation policy as an open-ended phenomenon, where three levels are interwoven and shape one another.

ARGUMENTS

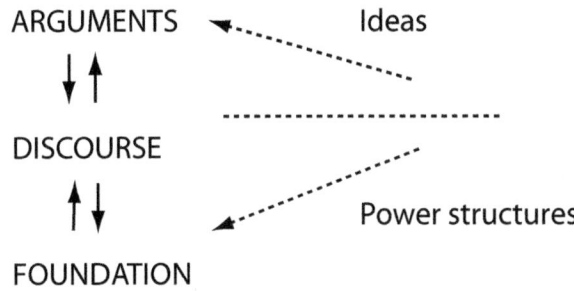

DISCOURSE

FOUNDATION

Figure 8.1 National identity as a discursive order

The findings in this study, using this model, underline that the foundation, the discourse and the arguments should be seen as levels, where the first is open to the influence of material power structures in society, and arguments to ideas. The discourse is the pattern in which these forces are shaped and reproduced. If the discourse is changed or expanded, innovations can be introduced from either the top (ideas) or the bottom (power structures). A prerequisite for change, however, is that neither of the foundations is being challenged. An individual who is acting strategically can through new ideas bring new arguments into the discourse, as long as they are compatible with existing foundations.[218] Or it may be possible to challenge the foundations through an expanded or transformed discourse. Another way of revising or expanding the discourse is by altering the power structures. By altering material resources, since power is reproduced through material capabilities, the discourse can be revised, allowing for the introduction of new arguments. Discourse is therefore the key concept in my definition of national identity.

217 Berger & Luckmann 1967 recalled these issues in social sciences. For a discussion consult Hollis 1994. Compare though Quine 1996.
218 Compare Checkel 1997b and the policy entrepreneurs who are dependent of the internal structure of the state. See also Demker 1998a.

The three levels – foundation, discourse and argument – can be studied both on the basis of their manifestations and their content.[219] It is through a dialogue between manifestation and content that national identity takes form and operates as the determinant of policy outcomes. In this study, I have argued that national identity is found in power relations, discourse/practice and rhetoric content.

I have also chosen to discuss national identity in terms of self-image. Self-image is in my view a manifestation of the national identity. Self-image has been analysed in terms of the perception of France, the perception of national community and the perception of national values. I have argued that these perceptions provide a broad picture of national identity as a concept founded on the distinction between "us" and "them". The distinction between us and them here is derived from the deconstructivist idea of "difference", introduced by Jacques Derrida.[220] What is present also contains what is not present. A dialectical process of sorts occurs in the construction of a national identity, and I have sought to analyse the nature of this dialectic. It is not a Hegelian dialectic, where all phenomena create their own opposite, but instead a dialectic that keeps together two counterparts within the same concept, where one is present and defined, and the other not present and undefined.[221]

The concept of national identity is often nebulous. In their evaluation of constructivist research, Martha Finnemore and Kathryn Sikkink state that "there is still no clear, agreed-on definition of what we mean (and do not mean) by identity".[222] Finnemore and Sikkink discuss the research on the mechanisms of identity construction. In this study, I believe I have uncovered a number of the mechanisms that change or transform identity conceptions. Power is one of the most neglected mechanisms in constructivist research. As Janice Bially Mattern points out in a review of a work on security communities by two of the most prominent constructivist scholars, these scholars (Adler and Barnett), like most of the constructivist thinkers, "exclude any significant role for power in the maintenance of community identity".[223] I propose a definition of national identity where innovations can come either from the top (ideas) or from the bottom (power).

---

219 Doty 1996:9. A manifestation could be the presence of something absent. This 'something' is there through its representation.
220 For ex Derrida 2000.
221 Hall 2000, Demker 2004.
222 Finnemore and Sikkink 2001:399
223 Bially Mattern 2000:304. Compare Guzzini 2000.

Power cannot on its own alter a national identity, but it constrains the opportunity for change. New ideas can be introduced through new arguments in the discourse and thereby expand or transform the discourse, but not if the power structures are challenged in the process. Altered power structures can be introduced, however, if they are possible to reproduce in the discourse and therefore give room for new arguments. Discourse is therefore the principal battleground for changing or transforming national identity. National identity is shaped through a discursive battle. It is of course not possible to simply step outside of the discourse. But by being aware and conscious of the discourse, one creates the possibility for its transformation.

8.3 How can national identities influence foreign policy?

I have argued that national identities are often the undisputed common ground for foreign policy. It is on the basis of national identity, in the discursive sense discussed above, that foreign policy decisions are made. Normally, national identity plays no apparent role because it is broadly accepted and simply reproduced through policy-making. But in times of foreign-policy uncertainty, of national crises, and of new and complex situations, national identity often becomes the determining, and conservative, factor. This does not mean that a given national identity must result in a specific outcome in foreign policy, but rather that some outcomes are impossible given a specific national identity.[224] National identity discourse is therefore both a restriction and a condition for national foreign-policy formulation. The rational preferences are therefore made on the basis of such identity conceptions. When the debate between France and United States about the intervention in Iraq 2003 was as most harsh, conceptions of their own national identity played a crucial role. The arguments about chemical weapons and how international law was to be interpreted were constituted by conceptions of France and USA. The implication for studies of international politics is that the national identity conception is founded on power relations, which represent and reproduce the structures of power resources within the national community. A perspective that has not been integrated in constructivistic studies – and a perspective that could make ends meet for both rationalists and constructivists.

224 Barnett 1999:26 argues that "constructivist scholarship ... needs to provide a fuller account of ... particularly strategic behaviour that is intended to alter the underlying rules of normative structures ...". See also Kaarbo 2003.

In the period under study, military authorities were quite powerful in France. They came to play a crucial role when the political system proved unable to bring stability to the national community. The same could be said about traditionally powerful groups such as wine producers and the industrial working class. In a society where the cleavages run deep, as they did in France at that time, and which is witnessing the transformation of its global role, polarised conflicts come to determine foreign policy. This blocking hindered, during the 1950s, both French peaceful decolonisation and a European integration process with France as a driving force.

National identity conceptions therefore are prominent factors for understanding and explaining foreign policy outcomes. Not because they necessarily determine the outcome, but because they at least restrain it. A state cannot choose its foreign policy rationally, as an actor on a free market. The choices confronting France in the decolonisation process – maintaining a global presence through its colonial empire or restricting itself to the European scene – could not be assessed freely and deliberately. The choice could not be made on the basis of values, despite that the human-rights regime created after the Second World War might have provided a justification for withdrawing from the colonies. France was restricted in its choices because of a discourse on national identity that, amid an identity crisis, could not simply be changed, challenged or expanded. The cross-pressure from the need for change (with the colonies and the war draining the economy and therefore preventing welfare reforms), and the incapacity of the system to bring about the needed change, in the end laid the foundations for a political collapse. Out of this chaos emerged Charles de Gaulle, bringing new power structures with him, such as an entirely new party organisation with broad popular support, as well as the natural military authority to make the difficult decision to withdraw and surrender.

My argument here is that an identity crisis does not necessarily help to create a new national identity; neither does it make it more plausible that a prevailing national identity will be challenged. In fact, although transforming the identity may seem the rational way to manage the situation, an identity crisis will in reality impede the process.[225] In the literature about policy entrepreneurs, identity change and ideas, it is often argued that so-called formative moments occur in times of crisis.[226] Finnemore and Sikkink state that research on ideas usually stipulates that situations, which are very complex or uncertain, are more open to the influence of

---

225 Sundelius et al 1997.

226 Ringmar 1996. The concept "formative moment" is a key concept in the new institutionalism.

new ideas.²²⁷ In his study about the end of the Cold War, Jeffrey Checkel highlights windows of opportunity where norm entrepreneurs can launch new ideas.²²⁸ Erik Ringmar, in a study on the participation of Sweden in the Thirty Years' War, argues that periods of uncertain national identity can lead to foreign policy adventures aimed at obtaining recognition and acceptance of a national identity.²²⁹ It is not that these scholars necessarily are mistaken in their analysis. There is, however, another angle on this issue, which I have brought to light in this study.

Because national identities are always present (they are not 'found' or 'discovered') they evolve as a perpetual sequence of manifestations, a dialectic between the present and the not present.²³⁰ What is inherent to national identity may in the next moment not be so. And what is not inherent was nonetheless present from the start. There is a constant process of distinctions and parting, where the discourse is the key since it is the battleground for how and whether the national identity is reproduced. National identity therefore cannot readily be transformed in times of crisis – quite the opposite. In times of international crisis, there is a need for decisions. But if the foreign policy elite are not capable of reaching a decision which is in line with the identity discourse, the decision will be illegitimate or impossible. Crises therefore do nothing to facilitate the transformation of national identity.

8.4 Epilogue

In his discussion of linguistics and the works of Martin Heidegger, Richard Rorty said that "Dasein (being) was linguistic through and through, just as it was social through and through."²³¹ This is the perspective that I propose be applied to the study of national identity.

According to Heidegger, the world in which we live is genuinely penetrated by our selves, and we are constituted along with the world.²³² Our life and our world are lived experiences, rather than objective realities. Heidegger challenges the view of the world as fact, as an empirical reality. In a factual world, human beings are to bend and adapt to the material

---

227 Finnemore and Sikkink 2001:406.
228 Checkel 1997a.
229 Ringmar 1996.
230 Doty 1996:169–170.
231 Rorty 1993:339.
232 Demker 2003 for a discussion.

circumstances. This is what Charles Taylor calls a "disengaged" position, in contrast with Heidegger's "engaged" position.[233] The point is that a so-called disengaged view of the world is, according to Heidegger, a turn away from our selves. The only way of being in the world is to be engaged. We know things as parts of a whole, we are involved in them and they are constituted by our very engagement. Engagement is understood as care ("die Sorge") in relation to our being in the world. Things in the world are then revealed to us as they are used and understood. And the others in the social world are revealed as a part of our selves.[234] This perspective gives strength to the constructivist premise in the social sciences, underlining that there is no neutral, objective standpoint from which we can observe our world.

The view of national identity as a contingent and discursive concept is built on the assumption that the social world is constituted by our common understanding of it. This assumption is, of course, neither testable nor subject to empirical research.[235] Our efforts to understand the world as we are thrown into it, and as it is given to us, makes it more or less plausible that the relevant world is constituted by our general social comprehension and not by material facts or objective knowledge. That does not mean that there is no material world, but that the material world is not the most relevant factor in understanding and explaining human behaviour.

It is interesting to note that it was in the 1950s, in France, that existentialism emerged. Albert Camus wrote his "Le mythe de Sisyfos" in 1942 and his other philosophical masterpiece, "L'homme revolté," in 1951, after breaking with Jean-Paul Sartre. Sartre, Simone de Beauvoir and many others re-discovered Martin Heidegger and developed a secular philosophy founded on the notions of human engagement and responsibility. The debate was especially intense during the Algerian War. In the pro-Mendès France news magazine L'Express, which where Mendès France's friend Jean-Jacques Servan-Schreiber served as editor and Albert Camus as journalist, an article about Heidegger, by Jacques Howlett, appeared on January 29, 1959. I would like to quote a short passage from the article:

> La condition de possibilité du souci c'est le temps. Avec le temps se découvre l'horizon à partir duquel se dévoile l'être de l'homme.[236]

---

233 Taylor 1993:333.
234 Heidegger 1927/1993, for commentaries Dreyfus 1991, Steiner 1997.
235 Hay 2002:34.
236 The condition for the possibility of care (die sorge) is time. In time is shown the horizon from which human spirit reveals itself.

This sentence means that time and context interplay to create new opportunities for individuals – opportunities that both constitute and are constituted by care (die Sorge) for one another and for the world.

Pierre Mendès France acted in the social temporal world, and his work and efforts should be interpreted inside that world. Had he succeeded in changing or expanding the discourse of national identity in France, the world might today have been otherwise. Mendès France acted in the world on the basis of that care for the being-in-the-world, he thought that the world could be otherwise and that it was his duty to reveal it as it could be. As human beings we are left with the world as we have made it, and were it not for the life of Mendès France, the world may not have been ready for the change, when it finally did come.

Archives: Consulted primary sources

UNIVERSITY LIBRARY OF GÖTEBORG UNIVERSITY

Section: Kurs och Tidningsbiblioteket, Göteborg

– *Le Monde* from 1953-06-01 until 1955-03-31
– *Le Figaro* front pages from 1954-12-01 until 1954-12-31
– *Dagens Nyheter* front pages from 1954-12-01 until 1954-12-31

Section: Centralbiblioteket, Göteborg

L'Année politique, Presses Universitaires de France, Paris, volumes:
– 1949
– 1950
– 1951
– 1952
– 1953
– 1954
– 1955
– 1956

INSTITUT PIERRE MENDÈS FRANCE, PARIS

Dossier Georges Bourdat volumes:
– BOU 2
– BOU 3
– BOU 4
– BOU 6

Dossier Jacques Legré volumes:
– Leg 1
– Leg 2
– Leg 4

Dossier Pierre Soudet volumes:
– SOU 4
– SOU 5

Dossier Pierre Mendès France volumes:
– TOM/Union Française
– Cabinet I
– Cabinet II (including calendrier 1954–1955)
– Afrique du Nord/Gouvernement Guy Mollet

Dossier Indochine volume I–IX

Dossier Algérie volume I–XIV

L'Express 1959-01-29 no 398 Jacques Howlett (Article about Heidegger)

References

Adler, Emanuel (1997) "Seizing the Middle Ground" *European Journal of International Relations* vol. 3 no. 3 p. 319–63.

Aimaq, Jasmine (1996) *For Europe or Empire. French colonial ambitions and the European army plan.* Lund University Press, Lund.

Aldrich Robert and John Connell (1998) *The Last Colonies.* Oxford University Press, Oxford.

Allan, Pierre (1994) "La complexité, le hasard et l'individu dans la théorie politique internationale" from Girard, Michel red. *Les individus dans la politique internationale*, Economica, Paris.

Allison, Graham T (1971) *Essence of decision. Explaining the Cuban missile crisis.* HarperCollins, New York.

Anderson, Benedict (1991) *Imagined communities. Reflections on the origins and spread of nationalism.* (revised version) Verso, London/New York.

Aussaresses, Paul (2001) *Services spéciaux. Algérie 1955-1957.* Perrin, Paris.

Azar, Michael (2001) *Frihet, Jämlikhet och Brodermord. Revolution och kolonialism hos Albert Camus och Franz Fanon* Symposion, Stehag/Stockholm.

Barnett, Michael (1999) "Culture, strategy and foreign policy change: Israel's road to Oslo" *European Journal of International Relations* vol. 5 1999 no. 1.

Bartelson, Jens (1997) "Identitet" from Goldmann, Kjell et al (ed) *Statsvetenskapligt Lexikon*, Universitetsförlaget, Stockholm.

— (2001) *The critique of the state*, Cambridge University Press, Cambridge.

Bédarida, François and Jean-Pierre Rioux (Ed) (1985) *Pierre Mendès France et le Mendésisme. L'Expérience gouvernemental (1954-1955) et sa postérité*, Fayard, Paris.

Berger, Peter L and Thomas Luckmann (1967) *The social construction of reality. A treatise in the sociology of knowledge.* Penguin books, Harmondsworth.

Berman, Sheri (2006) *The primacy of politics. Social democracy and the making of Europe's twentieth century*, Cambridge University Press, New York.

Berthier, Jean (1988) *Aide-mémoire d'histoire de France,* Bordas, Paris.

Braudel, Ferdinand (1969) *Écrits sur l'histoire*, Flammarion, Paris.

REFERENCES

Bring, Ove (1974) *Folkrätten och världspolitiken.* Askild & Kärnekull, Stockholm.

Brubaker, Rogers and Frederick Cooper (2000) "Beyond 'identity'" *Theory and Society,* vol. 29 no. 1 p. 1–47.

Bucken-Knapp, Gregg (2002) "Testing our borders: Question of national and regional identity in the Öresund region. *Journal of Baltic studies,* Vol. 33, no. 2 p. 199–219.

Burke, Peter (1992) *Annalesskolan. En introduktion.* Daidalos, Göteborg.

Busch, Peter (2003) *All the way with JFK? Britain, US and the Vietnam War,* Oxford University Press, Oxford.

Carlsson, Lars (2000) "Policy networks as collective action" *Policy Studies Journal,* vol. 28, no. 3 p. 502–520.

Chadwick, Andrew (2000) "Studying political ideas: a Public Political Discours Approach" *Political Studies,* vol. 48, nr 3, p. 283–301.

Chafer, Tony (2002) *The end of Empire in French West Africa. France's Successful Decolonisation?* Berg, Oxford.

Chamberlain, Muriel E. (1998) *The Longman companion to European decolonisation in the twentieth century,* Longman, London.

Checkel, Jeffrey (1997a) *Ideas and International Political Change. Soviet/Russian Behavior and the End of the Cold War,* Yale University Press, New Haven and London.

— (1997b) "International norms and domestic politics. Bridging the rationalist-constructivist debate" *European Journal of International Relations,* vol. 3, nr 4, p. 473–495.

Clayton, Anthony (1994) *The wars of French decolonisation.* Longman, London and New York.

Demker, Marie (1993) *I nationens intresse? Gaullismens partiideologi 1947–1990.* Nerenius & Santérus förlag, Stockholm.

— (1996) *Sverige och Algeriets frigörelse. Kriget som förändrade svensk utrikespolitik.* Nerenius & Santérus förlag, Stockholm.

— (1997) "Changing Party Ideology. Gaullist parties faces voters, organization and competitors" *Party Politics* vol. 3, no. 3.

— (1998a) "A Magic Moment in Swedish Foreign Policy: Voting Yes to Algerian Self-determination in 1959" *Cooperation and Conflict* vol.. 33, no. 2.

— (1998b) "Catholicism in the French electorate; Just ordinary conservative voters?" from Cooke, P. and K Chadwick ed. *Religion in modern and contemporary France,* Working papers on Contemporary France; volume 3, University of Portsmouth.

— (2003) *Att undersöka varandets vara. Några kunskapsteoretiska reflektioner över Martin Heideggers Varat och Tiden,* volym 1. Unpublished paper. Department of Philosophy, Göteborg University.

— (2004) "Självmordets dialektik. En studie av Kierkegaards 'Sjukdomen till döds'" *Filosofisk Tidskrift* vol. 25.

Derrida, Jacques (2000) "Signatur, händelse, kontext" from Marc-Wogau, Konrad; Lars Bergström and Staffan Carlshamre (ed) *Filosofin genom tiderna. Tiden efter 1950.* 2 ed., Thales, Stockholm.

Doty, Lynn Roxanne (1996) *Imperial encounters. The politics of representation in north-south relations.* University of Minnesota Press, Minneapolis.

— (1997) "Aporia. A critical exploration of the agent-structure problematique in international relations theory." *European Journal of International Relations* vol. 3, no. 3, pp 365–392.

Dreyfus, Hubert, L (1991) *Being-in-the-world. A commentary on Heidegger's Being and Time, division 1.* MIT Press, Cambridge, Mass.

Drulák, Petr (2006) "Motion, Container and Equilibrium: Metaphors in the Discourse about European Integration" *European Journal of International Relations*, vol. 12, no. 4, pp 499–531.

Eduards, Maud (1970) *Pierre Mendès France, son étiquette politique*, Trebetygs-uppsats, Department of French, Stockholm University, Stockholm.

Eisenhower, Dwight D (1963) *The White House Years: Mandate for change 1953–1956*. Heinemann, London.

Elgström, Ole (2000) *Images and strategies for autonomy. Explaining Swedish security policy strategies in the 19th century*. Kluwer Academic Publishers, Doordrecht/Boston/London.

Eriksson, Johan (1997) *Partition and redemption. A Machiavellian analysis of sami and basque patriotism*. Umeå University, Research report 1997:1 (Diss), Umeå.

Fink, Caroline (1989) *Marc Bloch. A life in history*. Cambridge University Press, Cambridge, UK.

Finnemore, Martha (1997) *National Interests in International Society*. Cornell University Press, Ithaca.

Finnemore, Martha and Kathryn Sikkink (2001) "Taking stock: The constructivist research program in international relations and comparative politics" *Annual Review of Political Science* vol. 4 p. 391–416.

Foucault, Michel (1970) *The order of things. An archaeology of the human sciences*. Vintage books, New York.

– (1971) *L'ordre du discours*. Gallimard, Paris.

George, Alexander (1980) *Presidential Decisionmaking in Foreign Policy: The Effective Use of Information and Advice*, Westview Press, Boulder, Colorado.

Geva, Nehemia and Alex Mintz ed (1997) *Decision making on War and Peace. The cognitive-Rational Debate*. Lynne Rienner Publishers, Boulder, Colorado.

Girard, Michel, editor (1999) *Individualism and World Politics*, Macmillan, Basingstoke and London.

Goldmann, Kjell (2001) *Transforming the European Nation-state. Dynamics of internationalization*. Sage, London.

Goldstein, Judith and Robert O. Keohane, ed. (1993) *Ideas and Foreign Policy. Beliefs, institutions and political change*. Cornell University Press, Ithaca.

Grendstad, Gunnar och Per Selle (1996) *Kultur som levemåte*. Det Norske Samlaget, Oslo.

Grosser, Alfred (1961) *La IVe république et sa politique extérieure*, Librairie Armand Colin, Paris.

Gustavsson, Jacob (1999) "How Should We Study Foreign Policy Change?" *Cooperation and Conflict*, vol. 34 no. 1.

Guzzini, Stefano (2000) "A reconstruction of constructivism in International relations" *European Journal of International Relations*, vol. 6, no. 2 p. 147–182.

Hajer, Maarten A (1995) *The politics if environmental discourse. Ecological Modernization and Policy Processes*. Oxford University Press, Oxford.

Hall, Ronald L. (2000) *The human embrace. The love of philosophy and the philosophy of love*. The Pennsylvania state university press, University Park, Pennsylvania.

Harmon, Hervé and Patrick Rotman (1979) *Les porteurs de valises. La résistance Française à la guerre d'Algérie*, Albin Michel, Paris.

Hay, Colin (2002) *Political Analysis. A critical introduction*. Palgrave, Basingstoke.

Heidegger, Martin (1927/1993) *Varat och tiden*. Vol. 1–2 *(Being and Time div 1–2)*. Daidalos, Göteborg.

Hollis, Martin (1994) *The philosophy of social science. An introduction.* Cambridge University Press, Cambridge.

Howarth, David, Aletta J. Norval and Yannis Stavrakakis (2000) *Discourse theory and political analysis. Identities, hegemonies and social change*, Manchester University Press, Manchester.

Hudson, Valerie M. ed. (1997) *Culture and Foreign Policy*, Lynne Rienner Publishers, Boulder London.

Jackson, Robert H. (1993) "The Weight of Ideas in Decolonization: Normative Change in International Relation" from Goldstein, J. and R. O. Keohane (ed) *Ideas and foreign policy. Beliefs, institutions and political change*, Cornell University Press, Ithaca.

Jackson, Thaddeus Patrick ed. (2004) "The Forum: Bridging the Gap: Toward a Realist-Constructivist Dialogue" *International Studies Review*, vo.l 6 no. 2 p. 337–352.

Joly, Danièle (1991) *The French communist party and the Algerian war.* Macmillan, London.

Jörgensen, Marianne Winther and Louise Philips (1999) *Diskursanalyse som teori og metode.* Roskilde Universitetsforlag/ Samfundslitteratur, Fredriksberg.

Kaarbo, Juliet (2003) "Foreign policy analysis in the twenty-first century: Back to comparison, forward to identity and ideas" *International Studies Review* vol. 5, 2003 p. 156–163.

Kahler, Miles (1984) *Decolonization in Britain and France. The domestic consequences of international relations.* Princeton University press, Princeton, NJ.

Katzenstein, Peter J. (1996) *The Culture of National Security. Norms and Identity in World Politics.* Columbia University Press, New York.

Klotz, Audie (1995) *Norms in international relations. The struggle against apartheid.* Cornell University Press, Ithaca.

Lacouture, Jean (1981) *Pierre Mendès France*, Seuil, Paris.

Larkin, Maurice (1997) *France since the popular front. Government and people 1936–1996.* Clarendon Press, Oxford (second edition).

Leclerc, Caroline (1984) *L'Express dans les années Mendès France ou la volonté de rajeunir la société Française*, Institut d'études politiques de Paris, Paris (Mémoire DEA).

Lundgren, Åsa (1998) *Europeisk identitetspolitik. EU:s demokratibistånd till Polen och Turkiet.* Skrifter utgivna av statsvetenskapliga föreningen i Uppsala. Almkvist och Wiksell International, Stockholm.

Prestre, Le Philippe ed. (1997) *Role Quests in the Post-Cold War Era. Foreign Policy in Transition*, McGills-Queens University Press, Quebec.

Mattern, Janice Bially (2000) "Taking identity seriously". *Cooperation and Conflict*, vol. 35, no. 3 p. 299–308.

— (2001) "The Power Politics of Identity" *European Journal of International Relations* vol. 7, no. 3, p. 349–397.

— (2005) *Ordering International Politics: Identity, Crisis and Representational Force.* Routledge, New York.

Mendès France, Pierre (1953) *Gouverner, c'est choisir. Discours d'Investiture et réponses aux interpellateurs.* René Juillard, Paris.

— (1984–1990) *Oeuvres complètes.* Gallimard, Paris.

— Vol. I *S'Engager 1922–1943* (1984)
— Vol. II *Une politique de l'économie 1943–1954* (1985)
— Vol. III *Gouverner, s'est choisir 1954–1955* (1986)
— Vol. IV *Pour une république moderne 1955–1962* (1987)

- Vol. V *Préparer l'avenir 1963-1973* (1989)
- Vol. VI *Une vision du monde 1974-1982* (1990)

Mendès France, Marie-Claire and Catherine David (1992) *L'esprit de liberté*, Presses de la Renaissance, Paris.

Mopin, Michel (1988) *Les grand débats parlementaires de 1875 a nos jours*. La Documentation Française, Paris.

Neu, Charles E. (2003) "Efforts to make sense of the Vietnam War". *Journal of Cold War Studies*, vol. 5 no. 2 p. 68-72.

Nye Jr, Joseph S. (1991) *Bound to lead. The changing nature of American power*. Basic Books/Harper Collins Publishers.

Oommen, T.K (1997) *Citizenship, nationality and ethnicity. Reconciling competing identities*. Polity Press, Cambridge.

Proust, Dominique (1984) *Pierre Mendès France et la Tunisie*, Institut de Sciences Politiques de Paris, Paris (Mémoire DEA).

Quine, Willard van Orman (1996) "Epistemology Naturalized" from Moser, Paul K (ed) *Empirical knowledge. Readings in contemporary epistemology*, Rowman & Littlefield Publishers, Lanham, Maryland.

Reclus, Philippe (1987) *La République impatiente ou Le Club des Jacobins (1951-1958)*, Publications de la Sorbonne, Paris.

Reitberger, Magnus (2000) *Consequences of contingency. The pragmatism and politics of Richard Rorty*. Department of political science, Stockholm University (Diss.).

Rhodes, Edward (1999) "Constructing power: Cultural Transforrmations and Strategic Adjustment in the 1890s" from Trubowitz, Peter, Emily O. Goldman and Edward Rhodes (ed) *The politics of strategic adjustment. Ideas, Institutions and interests*. Columbia University Press, New York.

Ringmar, Erik (1996) *Identity, Interest and Action. A cultural Explanation of Swedens's intervention in the Thirty Years War*, Cambridge University Press, Cambridge.

Rorty, Richard (1993) "Wittgenstein, Heidegger, and the reification of language" from Guignon, Charles B. *The Cambridge companion to Heidegger*, Cambridge University Press, Cambridge, UK.

Rothstein, Bo (2000) "Trust, social dilemmas and collective memories." *Journal of Theoretical Politics*, vol. 12 no 4 p. 477-501.

Searle, John R (1995) *The Construction of Social Reality*. Brockman Inc.

Shepard, Todd (2006) *The Invention of Decolonization: The Algerian War and the Remaking of France*, Cornell University Press, Ithaca.

Sikkink, Kathryn (1993) "The power of principled ideas: Human rights policies in the United States and Western Europe" from Goldstein J and R.O. Keohane (ed.) *Ideas and foreign policy. Beliefs, institutions and political change*, Cornell University Press, Ithaca.

Silverman, Maxim (1992) *Deconstructing the nation. Immigration, racism and citizenship in Modern France*. Routledge, London.

Singer, Eric and Valerie Hudson ed. (1992*) Political Psychology and Foreign Policy*, Westview Press, Boulder, CO.

Skinner, Quentin (1996) *Reason and rhetoric in the philosophy of Hobbes*. Cambridge University Press, Cambridge.

Smith, Anthony D. (1991) *National Identity*. Penguin books, London.

Stasse, François (2004) *L'héritage de Mendès France. Une étique de la république*, Seuil, Paris.

Steiner, Georg (1997) *Martin Heidegger. En introduktion*. Daidalos, Göteborg.

Stenlås, Niklas (1998) *Den inre kretsen. Den svenska ekonomiska elitens inflytande över partipolitik och opinionsbildning 1940-1949*. Arkiv Förlag, Bjärnum.

Sundelius, Bengt and Paul t'Hart, Eric Stern (1997) *Beyond groupthink. Political group dynamic and foreign policy making*. University of Michigan press, Ann Arbour.

Talbott, John (1980) *The war without a name. France in Algeria 1954-1962*. Faber and Faber, London.

Taylor, Charles (1993) "Engaged agency and background in Heidegger" from Guignon, Charles B. *The Cambridge companion to Heidegger*, Cambridge University Press, Cambridge, UK.

Tempelman, Sasja (1999) "Constructions of cultural identity: Multiculturalism and exclusion." *Political studies*, vol. 67, p. 17-31.

Thompson, Michael, Gunnar Grendstad & Per Selle ed. (1999) *Cultural Theory as political science*. Routledge, London.

Tralau, Johan (2001) *Människoskymning. Främlingskap, frihet – och Hegels problem hos Karl Marx och Ernst Jünger*. Brutus Östlings bokförlag Symposion, Stehag/Stockholm.

Tricot, Bernard (1972) *Les sentiers de la Paix. Algérie 1958-1962*. Plon Paris.

Tyre, Stephen (2006) "From Algerie Française to France Musulmane: Jacques Soustelle and the myths and realities of 'integration', 1955-1962" *French History*, September 2006.

Wardhaugh, Jessica (2007) "Fighting for the unknown soldier: The contested territory of the French nation in 1934-1938" *Modern & Contemporary France*, vol. 15, no. 2.

Wendt, Alexander (1999) *Social Theory of International Politics*, Cambridge University press, Cambridge.

Werth, Alexander (1957) *The strange story of Pierre Mendès France and the Great struggle over French-North Africa*, Harris, London.

Wertzberger, Yacov (1990) *The world in their minds. Information Processing, Cognition and Perception in Foreign Policy Decisionmaking*, Stanford University Press, Stanford.

Wesseling, H. L. (1997) *Imperialism and Colonialism. Essays on the History of European Expansion*. Greenwood Press, London.

Williams, Philip (1958) *Politics in postwar France. Parties and the constitution in the fourth republic*. Longmans, Green and Co, London/New York/Toronto.

Wilson, Richard W. (2000) "The many voices of political culture: Assessing different approaches" *World Politics* vol. 52 no. 2 p. 246-273.

Zehfuss, Maja (2001) "Constructivism and Identity: A Dangerous Liaison" *European Journal of International Relations* vol. 7 no. 3 p. 315-348.

INTERNET-REFERENCES

www.skalman.nu/vietnam 2003-05-08

The reader of this book may also be interested in:

Robert Dalsjö

Life-Line Lost

The Rise and Fall of 'Neutral' Sweden's Secret Reserve Option of Wartime Help from the West

Mikael Nilsson

Tools of Hegemony

Military Technology and Swedish-American Security Relations 1945–1962

Thomas Persson, Matti Wiberg (red)

Parliamentary Government in the Nordic Countries at a Crossroads

Coping with Challenges from Europeanisation and Presidentialisation

Read more and buy them at:

www.santerus.se

or at:

amazon.com

amazon.co.uk